MICHAEL MASSING

NOW
THEY
TELL
US

THE AMERICAN PRESS AND IRAQ

PREFACE BY OR

D1025356

as published in The New York Review of Books

NEW YORK REVIEW BOOKS, NEW YORK

THIS IS A NEW YORK REVIEW BOOK

PUBLISHED BY THE NEW YORK REVIEW OF BOOKS

NOW THEY TELL US: THE AMERICAN PRESS AND IRAQ
by Michael Massing

This edition published in 2004 in the United States of America by
The New York Review of Books, 1755 Broadway, New York, NY 10019
www.nybooks.com

Book and cover design by Milton Glaser, Inc.

Library of Congress Cataloging-in-Publication Data

Massing, Michael.
  Now they tell us / Michael Massing ; introduction by Orville Schell.
    p. cm.
  ISBN 1-59017-129-2 (pbk. : alk. paper)
  1. Iraq War, 2003 — Press coverage — United States. I. Title.
  DS79.76.M37 2004
  070.4'4995670443'0973 — dc22

                                        2004010496

ISBN 1-59017-128-4

Printed in the United States of America on acid-free paper.

July 2004

1 3 5 7 9 10 8 6 4 2

CONTENTS

PREFACE

WHEN ON MAY 26, 2004, the editors of *The New York Times* published their mea culpa apologizing for the paper's one-sided reporting on weapons of mass destruction and the Iraq war, it appeared as if they were responding directly to the issues raised months earlier in *The New York Review of Books* by Michael Massing, in articles now collected in this volume.

But while the *Times* editors admitted to "a number of instances of coverage that was not as rigorous as it should have been" and that they had since come to "wish we had been more aggressive in re-examining claims" made by the Bush administration, we are still left to wonder why the *Times*, like so many other major news organizations in this country, proved so lacking in skepticism toward official rationales for war. How could a policy that was based on such spurious exile intelligence sources and was so poorly conceived have been so blithely accepted, even embraced, by so many members of the American media? In short, what had happened to the press's vaunted role as skeptical "watchdog" over government power that our Founding Fathers had so carefully spelled out?

Answers, which became clearer as the war progressed and

Iraq fell into chaos, are alarming for what they now suggest about the cavalier and myopic way the officials of the Bush administration—whose members prided themselves on their acumen as skilled, no-nonsense corporate managers—did such a poor job of due diligence prior to their hostile takeover of Iraq. But just as alarming is the way the press, with a few notable exceptions, failed to respond first to the challenge of scrutinizing the administration's case for the war before the invasion and then its failures during and afterward.

It is understandable that governments should want to limit dissent within their own ranks and to avoid embarrassing disclosures. Less understandable, however, is that an independent press in a "free" country should allow itself to become so paralyzed that it not only failed to investigate thoroughly the rationales for war, but also took so little account of the myriad other cautionary voices in the on-line, alternative, and world press. Among the views and factual analyses that were largely ignored were those of multinational organizations, including the UN, where officials such as Mohamed ElBaradei, head of the International Atomic Energy Agency, and Hans Blix, head of the Monitoring, Verification and Inspections Commission, had a very different view of the Iraqi threat than the US government. Few, it seemed, remembered I. F. Stone's admonition,

"If you want to know about governments, all you have to know is two words: Governments lie."

For the most part, those dissenting voices in the US press that did speak out remained buried in the back pages of newspapers or confined to the margins of the media, unamplified through mass outlets in any meaningful way. They were thus denied the respectability that only inclusion in a major media outlet is capable of conferring on new information. As Massing points out, however, one large news organization, Knight Ridder, did consistently publish skeptical reports about administration claims concerning Iraq's weapons of mass destruction. But since the chain has no newspapers in New York and Washington, D.C., its reports were generally ignored among opinion-makers.

With few exceptions, the media of our country can be said to be divided into a two-tiered structure. The lower tier, populated by niche publications, alternative media outlets, PBS, NPR, and Internet sites, hosted the broadest spectrum of viewpoints. The upper tier, populated by the major broadcast outlets, newspapers, and magazines, allowed a much more limited bandwidth of opinion (often deferring to the Bush administration's vision of the world, especially on questions of war and peace) until the US occupation began to unravel in the spring of 2004. Only rarely were more contrarian views allowed to make their way upward from the lower to the upper tier.

As Michael Massing points out, one of the main factors that prevented a broader range of discussion on this upper tier and dissenting views from entering the bloodstream of the national discussion was insinuations by key US leaders that critics were lacking in patriotism. Such sentiments were made clear by the likes of White House Press Secretary Ari Fleischer, who, as the seemingly ineluctable war approached, infamously warned, "People had better watch what they say." Of course, such statements had a chilling effect on reporters, editors, news directors, publishers, and other kinds of media owners. The message coming out of the White House was: "If you are not with us, you are against us."

But other forms of pressure were also used to inhibit journalists. The President held few press conferences and rarely submitted to open questioning, so that even the White House press corps was rife with complaints about being shut out. Secretive and disciplined to begin with, the administration was also adept at using the threat of denied access as another means of bringing to heel reporters who evinced too much challenging independence. And for reporters, especially those covering the White House, no access means no one-on-one interviews, no special tips or leaks, exclusion from select events and important trips, and being passed over during question-and-answer periods at those few press conferences that do get held.

This bind was described to Massing by a US network correspondent who was reporting on the war from US Central Command headquarters at Doha, Qatar. "If she pushed too hard at the briefings," she told Massing, "she would no longer be called on."

Indeed, reports Massing, after the war began, Jim Wilkinson, a thirty-two-year-old Texan who ran CentCom's Coalition Media Center, "was known to rebuke reporters whose copy was deemed insufficiently supportive of the war" and "darkly warned one correspondent that he was on a 'list' along with two other reporters at his paper."

In other words, in the play-along/get-along world of the Bush administration, critical reporting was a quick ticket to access exile. Under such punitive circumstances, it was not easy for even experienced journalists to thoroughly perform their daily jobs, much less be challenging watchdogs.

The impulse to control the press did not, of course, originate with the administration of George W. Bush. But something did radically change during his tenure. Not only did his aides guard him carefully from unmediated exchanges with members of the press, but they marshaled enormous energy and resources to keeping control of his and other administration officials' message. The result was that until the press began to find a more independent voice again in the spring of 2004, the Bush propaganda machine was not only able to set the terms of discussion but to isolate and ignore "unfriendly" members of the press. The notion that the President or some other high official might vigorously defend the right of the press to challenge the government, even if that official disagreed with a reporter on a given policy, was almost an unthinkable one. Administration leaders were hardly inclined to echo Thomas Jefferson's famous declaration that "the basis of our government being the opinion of the people, the very first object should be to keep that right; and were it left to me to decide whether we should have a government without newspapers or newspapers without government, I should not hesitate a moment to prefer the latter."

One of the reasons that the Bush administration seems to have so little esteem for the watchdog role of the press is that its own conception of the "truth" has not always been derived from factual reality. Instead, it has embraced a new criterion for veracity, namely, "faith-based" truth—sometimes even corroborated by what has come to be known as "faith-based intelligence"—which bespeaks a truth that can literally be received from on-high as a kind of divine revelation that begs no further earthly scrutiny. President Bush was, for instance, reported in the Israeli paper *Haaretz* as having told Palestinian Prime Minister Mahmoud Abbas, "God told me to strike Al Qaeda and I struck, and then he instructed me to strike Saddam, which I did."

It is hardly surprising that he eschews newspapers and magazines in favor of reports from other more "objective sources," namely his staff, which he describes as "the most objective source I have." He has also frequently spoken of trusting "visceral reactions" or of acting on the basis of "gut feelings" rather than basing judgments on a careful study of the issues. "I'm not a textbook player," he told *The Washington Post*'s Bob Woodward in *Bush at War*. "I'm a gut player."

In any case, decision-making for George W. Bush does not necessarily proceed from evidence to conclusion, but often from conclusion to evidence. Reading, facts, history, logic, and the complex interaction between the electorate, media, and government seem to play a somewhat subsidiary role in such a process of "fundamentalist" policy formation.

Just as journalism and the free exchange of information may

play little part in the relationship between a believer and his or her God, so it may play a less important part in this parallel world of divine political revelation. After all, if one already knows the answer to a question, why pay heed to the press? For such a leader, the task is not so much to listen and learn, but to teach—to proselytize the received political gospel among nonbelievers, thus transforming the once interactive process between citizen and leader into a form of evangelism.

Although in this new political universe of faith-based truth, "freedom" is endlessly extolled in principle, it has little utility in practice. For what possible role can a free press play when revelation trumps fact and conclusions are preordained? In such an atmosphere, a probing press is quite naturally viewed as a spoiler, an uncooperative and unwelcome intruder confusing the minds of those whose only true salvation lies in becoming true believers.

Since there is little need, and less respect, for an opposition (loyal or otherwise), the process by which independently arrived-at information feeds back into government decision-making, a process in which the press plays a crucial role in any functioning democracy, ceases to operate. The crucial synapses which normally transmit warnings from citizen observers to government increasingly freeze shut. Television networks may continue to broadcast and newspapers may continue to publish, but if dismissed and ignored, they tend to become irrelevant, except possibly for their entertainment value. And should the members of the press involved arch their backs and become more critical in protest, they are pilloried as unduly "negative," denigrated as "bashers" of the nation's leaders, and discounted all the more. The result is that as the press withers, the government it covers, which may already have tendencies toward being self-referential and deluded by self-deception, ends up being deprived of one of the few institutional ways it can learn of danger and make course corrections. If this tendency continues uncorrected, one of the most elemental assumptions of our American republic, the idea that a free and independent press is a crucial way for ordinary citizens to be heard in the high councils of government, becomes inoperative.

As Andrew Card, the President's chief of staff, bluntly declared to *New Yorker* writer Ken Auletta, members of the press "don't represent the public any more than other people do.... I don't believe you have a check-and-balance function." Auletta, who has long followed the media, came to the extreme conclusion that in the eyes of the Bush administration, the press corps had become just another special-interest lobby group.

If, in fact, the media is being downgraded by our leaders

from its historic role as the "fourth estate" in our nation's system of checks and balances to just another special-interest lobbying group, what does this say about how our government views its citizens, the putative sovereigns of our country? It suggests that "we the people" are no longer seen so much as a political constituency conferring legitimacy on our rulers, but as something more akin to passive consumers of their political messages. The former needs to be become well-informed by means of accurate information and a wide variety of views so as to be able to choose its government representatives wisely. The latter needs to be controlled by massive doses of special interest–funded commercials and partisan propaganda so as not to disturb the status quo.

The influence of selling techniques developed by commercial advertisers attached to political campaigns is, of course, nothing new in American political life or the journalism that covers it. But the degree to which the political process has now become saturated with public relations, advertising artifice, amoral political consultants, and hired spin doctoring has reached an apogee in the past few years. The consequence of this trend is that "traditional" news outlets find themselves increasingly drowned out and ghettoized in preserves in which their mass appeal and influence is sharply diminished. Attacked as "liberal" and "elitist," dismissed as "troublemakers," and no longer even sustained by the once commonly shared presumption among the public that a free, aggressive, and iconoclastic press is a healthy thing for any free country, the major news organizations now sometimes seem to verge on becoming irrelevant. Being forced to work in such a climate, it is no small wonder, then, that members of the press have become so uncertain and timid about whether they have a legitimate place in the political process.

But as we contemplate the war in Iraq and the inadequate reporting of it so thoroughly documented by Michael Massing, there is another, even more damaging dynamic in evidence, one that intellectuals from Marxists-Leninist societies would instantly recognize. This is the psychological tendency of any group that is denied legitimacy and officially disdained by a powerful state to begin internalizing its sense of exclusion and isolation as a form of culpability, causing an almost autonomic urge to somehow seek out reinstatement. Especially among liberal democrats, in whom there is an ever-present instinct to evince fairness and reason, there is a strong tendency to want to show their goodwill and honorable intentions by presenting in a favorable light political positions about which they may actually have deep doubts. This is a tendency that often becomes all the stronger as a regime's criticism of the press becomes more harshly disparaging. Always wanting to appear fair-minded, liberal journalists paradoxically become all the more eager to please critics who bully them with accusations of being "unpatriotic" or "un-American."

With the new engines of ersatz news and information generated by political polemicists competing ever more aggressively for our media attention, the main ways that most Americans gain information about politics and politicians have changed dramatically. That territory the traditional media once occupied almost exclusively had, by the fall of 2003, been so intruded on by these new forms of political "communication" that were drenching media (especially broadcast) outlets with cleverly staged "photo ops," carefully produced propaganda rallies, tidal waves of campaign ads, and endless celebrity fund-raisers (from which reporters were usually excluded) that it was hard for anyone but true political savants to know what was real and what was not. The idea of a truly open press conference, an unscripted political debate, a leisurely and open on-stage conversation between political leaders, or even a one-on-one interview between a member of the press and an undefended politician had become almost quaint in conception.

After all, the current object of our political campaigns—which never seem to end—is not to inform or illuminate the public, but to sell a political position much the same way a corporation seeks to market a product. And, afraid of losing out on the lucrative ad revenues that come from such mass political image-making, major media outlets quietly yield rather than resist, and thus lose their skeptical, inquiring edge. It was little wonder, then, that "the traditional press" had a difficult time breaking through this multilayered defensive shield of intimidation and spin, much less standing up to the White House and providing a convincing counternarrative as the nation headed to war.

We are, in short, living at a time when the main informational gateway between citizens and political leaders is less and less the province of conventional news organizations and more and more the province of costly public relations and advertising campaigns paid for by political candidates and their polemicists. Not only has this new, mutant, and very partisan kind of skepticism-free "news" succeeded in leaving large segments of the populace uninformed, but since so much of it is unquestioning of conventional wisdom—or worse, simply repeats or "reports on" political propaganda—it has also corrupted the ability of high officials to see themselves clearly. In the end, they all too often find themselves looking into a mirror of their own making. As even the conservative *National Review* noted in an editorial, the Bush administration has "a dismaying capacity to believe its own public relations."

In this new world of "news," information loops have tended to become one-way highways. A national security adviser, cabinet secretary, or attorney general becomes not so much a conveyor of straightforward information, and certainly not a seeker of truth, but a well-managed, -programmed, and -funded polemicist whose charge is to "stay on message," the better to justify what the government has already done, or is about to do. All too many government officials have become salespeople.

Because these latter-day media campaigns that the press feels obliged to cover as "news" now employ all the sophistication and technology developed by communications experts since Edward Bernays, nephew of Sigmund Freud, first wed an understanding of human psychology and the marketing of merchandise to launch the PR revolution and our consumer society, they are far more seductive and effective than older-style "news." Indeed, in cable television networks like Fox, we see the ultimate marriage of news and PR to create a flow of guileful propaganda capable of creating a virtual world that is so well packaged and presented that most people have a difficult time understanding how false its representations actually are.

While governments have rarely ever welcomed critical reporting, few democratic governments have sought to undermine the philosophical underpinnings of a free and independent press. What is distinctive about the past four years is that we have been governed by a political leadership which views neither information nor debate as an indispensable element in the political process. Indeed, many of its key members do not even see the press as playing any constructive role at all. The principles of independent journalism that prize showing neither fear nor favor to any may remain enshrined in the rhetoric of many well-known newspapers and broadcasters. However, it may be that the political and commercial context in which the media must now operate has changed so radically that such journalism can no longer be counted on to serve as an independent and effective structural force in our society. This is perhaps the unspoken, if discouraging, subtext of Michael Massing's insightful original articles and the challenging epilogue he has added to them.

As the war in Iraq descended into a desert quagmire, the press belatedly appeared to wake up and adopt a more skeptical view of US policy. The circulation of photographs of tortured Iraqis probably had more of an effect than many millions of words. But if a bloody, expensive, and ill-advised war is required as a wake-up call to remind the media of its critical role as watchdog in the functioning of American democracy, it is hard to avoid the conclusion that something is gravely amiss in the way our political system has come to function.

—ORVILLE SCHELL

NOW
THEY
TELL
US

As published in *The New York Review of Books*
May 29, 2003

THE UNSEEN WAR

1. **THE COALITION MEDIA CENTER,** at the Saliyah military base in Doha, Qatar, seems designed to be as annoying and inconvenient as possible for reporters. To get there from the center of town, you have to take a half-hour ride through a baking, barren expanse of desert. At the gate, you have to submit your electronic equipment to a K-9 search, your bags to inspection, and your body to an X-ray scan. You then have to wait under the scorching sun for a military escort, who, after checking your credentials, takes you to the press bus. When the bus is full, you're driven the two hundred yards to the media center. The bus lets you off in a concrete courtyard surrounded by a seven-foot-high wall topped by barbed wire. If you stand on a ledge and look out, you'll see two rows of identical warehouse-like buildings—the offices of General Tommy Franks and the US Central Command.

Journalists, though, never get inside these buildings, for they're restricted to the windowless media center, which is sixty feet long, brightly lit, and heavily air-conditioned. Inside the front door is a large space with long counters at which reporters for second-tier news organizations work. Extending out from this area are three corridors housing the offices of the TV networks, wire services, and major newspapers. Along the back wall is the door to the UK press office. Knock on it and moments later an officer in fatigues will appear and field your request. By contrast, the door to the US office, to the right of the main entrance, opens onto an empty corridor, and if you knock on it no one will answer. Instead, you have to phone the office and leave your request with the officer on duty. If you're lucky, someone will come out and speak with you.

During the war, many of the reporters crammed into the center would dial the US number, seeking to check facts, get some background information, or ferret out a bit of news. Usually, they'd be disappointed. Getting confirmation for even the most basic facts filed by reporters in the field would often prove difficult. Occasionally, a senior press officer would emerge to speak with a reporter, and within minutes a ravenous mob would surround him, desperately seeking to shake loose something even remotely newsworthy.

The daily briefings were even less helpful. Held in a large conference hall with the now-famous $250,000 stage set, the briefings were normally conducted by Vincent Brooks, a tall, erect, one-star general who is impeccably polite, unflappable, and remarkably uninformative. Each briefing would begin with a few choice videos—black-and-white clips of "precision-guided" missiles unfailingly hitting their targets, and color shots of American troops distributing aid to grateful Iraqis. No matter what was taking place inside Iraq, Brooks would insist that the coalition remained "on plan" and that morale remained "sky high." Sometimes the general offered outright misinformation. When, for instance, the Palestine Hotel was hit by a US tank shell, which killed two journalists and wounded several others, Brooks asserted that US forces had come under fire from the hotel. This was denied by the journalists on the scene, and the commander of the unit that fired the shell, in an interview with *Le Nouvel Observateur*, made no mention of being fired on from the hotel. Still, Colin Powell, citing no evidence, later repeated the claim that "our forces responded to hostile fire, appearing to come from" the hotel.

The Coalition Media Center is managed by Jim Wilkinson, a fresh-faced, thirty-two-year-old Texan and a protégé of Bush adviser Karen Hughes. Wilkinson made his mark during the 2000 presidential election when he spoke on behalf of GOP activists protesting the Florida ballot recount. To run the media center in Doha, Wilkinson, a member of the naval reserve, appeared in the same beige fatigues as the career officers working under him. Nonetheless, the center had all the ear-marks of a political campaign, with press officers always "on message." Many journalists, accustomed to the smoothly purring Bush political machine, were struck by the heavy-handedness of the Doha operation. A week into the war, jour-nalists began writing their own "media pieces," as they called them, comparing the briefings to the infamous "Five O'Clock Follies" of the Vietnam War.

Rarely, though, did those stories examine how well the press, radio, and television themselves were doing, and that was unfortunate. For, with more than seven hundred registered journalists, the Coalition Media Center offered a superb oppor-tunity for observing how reporters of different nations approached the war, and for understanding the many short-comings in their coverage.

SO STINGY IS CENTCOM WITH INFORMATION THAT, at the daily briefings, the questions asked were often more revealing than the answers given. Those posed by European and Arab journalists tended to be more pointed and probing than those from the Americans. The Europeans and Arabs would ask about the accuracy of US missiles, the use of weapons containing depleted uranium, the extent of civilian casualties. The Americans would ask questions such as: "Why hasn't Iraqi broadcasting been taken out?" "Is Iraq using weapons prohibited by the UN?" "Can you offer more details on the rescue of Jessica Lynch?" One US network correspondent told me that she was worried that, if she pushed too hard at the briefings, she would no longer be called on. Jim Wilkinson was known to rebuke reporters whose copy he deemed insufficiently supportive of the war; he darkly warned one correspondent that he was on a "list" along with two other reporters at his paper.

After each briefing, correspondents for the major satellite networks would stand up in back and give a live report before a camera. Sometimes I took a seat nearby and listened. The British correspondents invariably included some analysis in their reports. After one briefing, for instance, James Forlong of Sky News observed that Tommy Franks had left the briefing to his "fourth in command" (i.e., Brooks), and that "very little detail had been provided." Referring to a question about a friendly-fire incident, Forlong noted that Brooks had little to say other than that the incident was "under investigation." CNN's Tom Mintier, by contrast, would faithfully recite Brooks's main points, often with signs of approval. "They showed some amazing footage of a raid on a palace," he said when introducing a clip that had been shown at the briefing, one of many that CNN aired.

Such differences in style were apparent in the broadcasts themselves. Switching stations in my hotel, I often found myself drawn to the BBC. With two hundred reporters, producers, and technicians in the field, its largest deployment ever, the network offered no-nonsense anchors, tenacious correspondents, perceptive features, and a host of commentators steeped in knowledge of the Middle East, in contrast to the retired generals and colonels we saw on American TV. Reporters were not afraid to challenge the coalition's claims. When an anchor asked Paul Adams, a BBC defense correspondent, whether Iraqi fighters were using "quasi-terrorist tactics"—a common Centcom charge—he said it was more appropriate to speak of "asymmetrical warfare," i.e., the use of unconventional tactics by forces that were badly outgunned. At the same time, the BBC presented many stories about the horrors of Saddam's rule. In one chilling piece, it had an interview with an Iraqi woman in London whose family members had been murdered, raped, or tortured by the regime.

At times, the BBC seemed relatively slow and ponderous. When the tape of Saddam's appearance in the streets of Baghdad was shown on al-Jazeera, the BBC took ten minutes longer than other networks to air it. A feature about Günter Grass and his visceral hatred for America seemed to be repeated endlessly. All in all, though, the BBC maintained a consistent standard of skepticism toward all sides. "We're very conscious that our audience is not just a coalition audience but an international one," Jonathan Marcus, a correspondent for BBC Radio, told me. "Tone, style, and terminology are all employed with that very much in mind. That has sharpened our journalism enormously."

The BBC got some stiff competition from Sky News. With a much smaller staff than the BBC, this London-based channel (partly owned by Rupert Murdoch) seemed far more nimble. One of its correspondents, Geoff Meade, became known at the media center for his sharp, if sometimes grandiloquent, questions. When Baghdad was about to fall without the discovery of any weapons of mass destruction, he asked, "Is this war going to make history by being the first to end before its cause could be found?" Among Sky's regular commentators, Con Coughlin, a biographer of Saddam and a *Daily Telegraph* editor, explained how Baath Party loyalists would likely have been recruited to play a part in Saddam's allegedly spontaneous street appearances.

After watching the British reports, I found the American ones jarring. In my hotel, MSNBC always seemed to be on, and I was shocked by its mawkishness and breathless boosterism. Its anchors mostly recounted tales of American bravery and derring-do. After the US attacks on the Palestine Hotel and the offices of al-Jazeera in Baghdad, MSNBC brought on its resident terrorism expert, Steve Emerson, who insisted—before any of the facts were in—that the attacks were accidental. MSNBC's "embedded" reporters, meanwhile, seemed utterly intoxicated by the war. In one tendentious account, Dr. Bob Arnot—normally assigned to the health beat—excitedly followed his cameraman into an unlighted building where two captured Iraqi fighters were being held near the entrance while a group of women and children could be seen in back. "They're fighting outside," Arnot said with indignation. "Here in the front are RPGs [rocket-propelled grenades] used to kill Marines, and in the back are these women and children— civilian hostages. And they're terrified." But terrified of what?

The captured men in the front room? The fighting outside? Were they being held against their will? Arnot never asked.

Before arriving in Doha, I had spent hours watching CNN back home, and I was sadly reminded of the network's steady decline in recent years. Paula Zahn looked and talked like a cheerleader for the US forces; Aaron Brown kept reaching for the profound remark without ever finding it; Wolf Blitzer politely interviewed Washington's high and mighty, seldom asking a pointed question. None of them, however, appeared on the broadcasts I saw in Doha. Instead, there were Jim Clancy, a tough-minded veteran American correspondent, Michael Holmes, a soft-spoken Australian, and Becky Anderson, a sharp and inquisitive British anchor. This was CNN International, the edition broadcast to the world at large, and it was far more serious and informed than the American version.

The difference was not accidental. Six months before the war began, I was told, executives at CNN headquarters in Atlanta met regularly to plan separate broadcasts for America and the world. Those executives knew that Zahn's girl-next-door manner and Brown's spacey monologues would not go down well with the British, French, or Germans, much less the Egyptians or Turks, and so the network, at huge expense, fielded two parallel but separate teams to cover the war. And while there was plenty of overlap, especially in the reports from the field, and in the use of such knowledgeable journalists as Christiane Amanpour, the international edition was refreshingly free of the self-congratulatory talk of its domestic one. In one telling moment, Becky Anderson, listening to one of Walter Rodgers's excited reports about US advances in the field, admonished him: "Let's not give the impression that there's been no resistance." Rodgers conceded that she was right.

CNN International bore more resemblance to the BBC than to its domestic edition—a difference that showed just how market-driven were the tone and content of the broadcasts. For the most part, US news organizations gave Americans the war they thought Americans wanted to see.

3.

EVEN THE MOST INTERNATIONALLY MINDED WESTERN NEWS organizations, however, faced serious problems in covering the war. In Doha, most journalists spent their days shuttling between the Coalition Media Center and their plush five-star hotels. Had the journalists taken the time to look around Qatar itself, they would have witnessed a fascinating political experiment. Though slightly smaller than Connecticut, Qatar sits on enough natural gas to heat every home in America for more than one hundred years, and its emir, Hamad bin Khalifa al-Thani, is trying to use that wealth to create a modern society that he thinks could be a model for the Arab world. During my stay, Qatar took a step toward democracy by holding municipal elections, and among the winners was a woman—one of the first to be elected to public office in the Gulf. In Doha's spotless shopping malls, men in white robes and black headbands line up for Starbucks coffee and Subway sandwiches, an example of the combination of Wahhabi austerity and Western consumerism that is apparent throughout the country.

Few journalists, though, got to see it. Working late into the night to accommodate editors seven time zones away, they got most of their information about the outside world from TV, the Internet, and their colleagues in the field. Talking with them at the media center and the Sheraton and Ritz-Carlton, I found

13

that they were mainly concerned with such military matters as troop deployments, tank formations, and the length of supply lines. Since the journalists were in Doha to cover Centcom, these concerns were natural, but the reporters for the most part seemed unconcerned about the political aspects of the military campaign—for instance, the workings of the Baath Party police; the attitudes of the different parts of Saddam's armed forces toward his dictatorship; the interests and resentments of the various Islamic groups and their leaders.

Part of the difficulty was that the reporters knew very little about the Middle East. Most had come to Doha from bureaus far afield—Washington, Mexico City, Rome, Brussels, Nairobi, Bangkok, Hong Kong. They were unfamiliar with Arab history, the roots of Islamic fundamentalism, the resurgence of Arab nationalism, the changes in the regional balance of power since September 11. Particularly serious was their lack of knowledge of Arabic. They could not talk with Arabic speakers directly, read Arabic newspapers, or watch Arabic news channels.

For American TV networks, the lack of experience in the Middle East reflects a turning away from the world that has been going on for a long time. Tom Fenton of CBS told me that when he joined the network, in 1970, "I was one of three correspondents in the Rome bureau. We had bureaus in Paris, Bonn,

Warsaw, Cairo, and Nairobi. Now you can count the number of foreign correspondents on two hands and have three fingers left over. Before, we had stringers all over the world. Now no one can afford that." Even *The Washington Post* has only a handful of people fluent in Arabic, and only one of them—Anthony Shadid—was stationed inside Iraq. Because of his knowledge of the region and its language he was one of the few US correspondents able to get beneath the surface of life in Baghdad.

Many reporters lacked even the most rudimentary knowledge of Iraqi history and geography. A correspondent for the *Los Angeles Times* told me of a gung-ho colleague who, embedded with a Marine unit that was racing toward Baghdad, excitedly declared over the phone, "We're about to cross the Ganges!" When he was told that he must mean the Tigris, he said, "Yeah, one of those biblical rivers or other." When I mentioned to a reporter for *USA Today* how hard it seemed to cover the Middle East without much experience in the region, she was dismissive. "You can read one book, like *God Has Ninety-Nine Names*, and figure out what's going on here," she said, referring to the 1996 book by Judith Miller. "You can talk to any cabdriver and he'll tell you everything you need to know." As it happens, most of the cab drivers in Doha are from India and Pakistan.

PROBABLY THE BIGGEST PROBLEM for journalists unfamiliar with the region and its language was their inability to tune in to Arabic-language newscasts. During the first Gulf War, there were no all-news Arabic channels, and Arabs, like everyone else, had to rely on CNN. Now there are many such channels. The newest, the Saudi-backed al-Arabiya, went on the air just weeks before the start of the war. The most important, however, remains al-Jazeera. Even before the war, it had an estimated 35 million viewers; after its start, the number of its subscribers in Europe jumped by 50 percent. If you walk into a working-class café in the Arab world, chances are it will have a TV tuned to al-Jazeera. It has been central in defining how Arabs have seen the war.

For those in the West who get to see it, al-Jazeera remains an enigma. On the one hand, it has run lengthy interviews with US officials like Donald Rumsfeld and Richard Myers; during the war, it stayed with the Pentagon's briefings long after other networks had gotten bored and moved on. Al-Jazeera has offended many Arab governments with its frank coverage of their repressive policies. During the war Iraqi Information Minister Muhammed Saeed al-Sahaf denounced it for "marketing to America."

At the same time, al-Jazeera has aired unedited tapes from Osama bin Laden, and many who followed its reports from

Afghanistan during the war there felt it had a decidedly pro-Taliban tilt. It has shown hours of coverage of Palestinian casualties in the West Bank and Gaza and commonly refers to suicide bombers as martyrs. A week into the war in Iraq, it broadcast a tape of US POWs being interrogated and another of dead British soldiers, and it was rebuked for doing so by the brass of both nations.

A visit to al-Jazeera's central studios, in Doha, is instructive. Built with a $140 million grant from the emir of Qatar, they are as advanced as any Western network's, with a sleek, airy newsroom in which a wall of monitors shows satellite feeds from around the world. On its staff are people of eighteen nationalities, including displaced Palestinians and Lebanese Christians. Some of the men wear sports shirts and slacks, the women jeans and sandals. Jihad Ballout, al-Jazeera's new press spokesman, appears in a leather jacket, smokes Gitanes, and drives a BMW convertible. But here, too, are women in traditional black robes and men in traditional white ones; among the latter is the channel's chairman, Sheik Hamad bin Thamer al-Thani, a member of Qatar's royal family.

In fact, as I learned in Doha, al-Jazeera's staff has two main factions. One, the Islamists, subscribe to a form of religion-based Arab nationalism, which strongly opposes Western culture and Western political power. The other, the secularists, are drawn to liberalism and modernism, and some have close contacts in Europe. The two groups are engaged in a struggle for power. Riad Kahwaji, the Middle East bureau chief of *Defense News*, told me that he thought the dispute within al-Jazeera reflected "a broader struggle within the Arab world." Before the collapse of the Soviet Union, he said, political opinion in the Arab world could, very roughly speaking, be seen as divided between the "traditional left," often secular, and the "traditional right," sometimes religious. With the Soviet collapse, however, the left largely disappeared, as it did in Egypt, and the vacuum was increasingly filled by hard-line Islamists. Governments, forced to respond, have themselves more and more adopted Islamist positions. As a result, the region's politics have become saturated with religion. "This has had an influence on everything—especially the media," Kahwaji said. "And al-Jazeera is no exception."

As I learned from people familiar with the station, there is little doubt that the Islamists and those vehemently opposed to the West have the upper hand. And this was certainly borne out when, helped by Arabic translators, I watched the channel. Occasionally there appeared a moderate Arab expressing hopes for a democratic Iraq. Mostly, though, I heard expressions of anti-Western Arab nationalism. Much was made of a pro-Saddam demonstration in Mosul. Saudi scientists urged Arabs to protest the war. Iraqi citizens were shown rejoicing at the destruction of an American tank. Usually, the coalition was referred to as an invading or occupying force, with hardly any indication that it was also opposing a particularly cruel dictatorship.

Several times an hour, we saw footage of civilian casualties. Al-Jazeera took us to hospital wards to show us screaming children, women in pain, men without limbs. The camera lingered on stumps, head wounds, and tubes inserted in nostrils and chests. On gurneys in hallways lay bodies bandaged, bloodied, and burned. Doctors and nurses described how they were being overwhelmed by casualties and how they lacked the supplies needed to treat them. (As Tim Judah wrote in *The New York Review*, many of the casualties were in fact military.[1])

On al-Jazeera, then, the war was seen mainly through the plight of its victims, while the brutality of the Baathists and their horrifying methods were hardly mentioned. And other Arabic newscasts did not look much different. Al-Arabiya, which is casting itself as a moderate alternative to al-Jazeera, also heavily featured civilian casualties. In doing so, both channels reflected popular sentiment in the region. "The overwhelming majority of the Arab world does not believe the US invasion is legitimate," Riad Kahwaji observed. "They regard the US presence in Iraq as an illegal occupation." In short, the war has helped to solidify Islamist tendencies in the Middle East, and this development has been reflected in—and reinforced by— the Arab press and television.

5.

TO ME, THE WAR AS SHOWN on al-Jazeera seemed one-sided; its coverage would have benefited from more reports on Saddam's crimes and the opposition to him from the Shiite majority and from many other elements in the population. Yet Western television programs seemed to tilt in the opposite direction, showing a war of liberation without victims. The more than five hundred reporters embedded with military units provided some unforgettable glimpses of the war, but remarkably few showed war's real-life effects, i.e., people getting killed and maimed.

Consider, for example, the day on which US troops made their initial raid inside Baghdad. The fighting was so intense that, according to Centcom, between two thousand and three thousand Iraqi soldiers died. Yet, on TV, I didn't see a single one of them. On MSNBC, the anchor announced that its live video feed was being put on five-second delay so that images deemed too "disturbing" could be weeded out. On CNN the only casualty I saw was when Walter Rodgers and his crew found an Iraqi soldier lying wounded on the side of the road. A CNN security officer who had some medical training stopped to help the man while US Army medics were summoned. This made for dramatic TV, and it showed the type of casualties CNN apparently thought appropriate for broadcast—those assisted by compassionate Americans.

In Qatar, the *International Herald Tribune* comes with a regionally produced insert, *The Daily Star*, and it was revealing to compare the two. Here, for instance, are some of the headlines that appeared in the *Herald Tribune* on April 7:

RECOGNIZING THE VICTORY: HOW WILL US KNOW WHEN IT HAS WON THE WAR IN IRAQ?

FOR US SOLDIERS, THERAPY HELPS EASE BATTLE STRESS

HOPE FOR MISSING GI'S GIVES WAY TO SADNESS

RESCUED US PRIVATE REUNITED WITH FAMILY

That same day, *The Daily Star* carried a front-page story headlined IRAQI HOSPITALS OFFER SNAPSHOT OF HORROR. It began with the ordeal of Ali Ismail Abbas, the twelve-year-old Baghdad boy who lost his family and both his arms in a US missile attack. It went on to describe how the staff at the hospital he'd been brought to "were overwhelmed by the sharp rise in casualties since American troops moved north to Baghdad Thursday and intensified their aerial assault." I found hardly any mention of this in the *Herald Tribune* on that day.

Such differences, I was told in Doha, reflect not only the widespread opposition to the war in the Middle East but also the fact that people there have much greater tolerance for graphic images than do those in the United States. American movies feature scenes of people being blown up and gunned down; American TV programs show women being slashed and men being shot in the face. But television executives believe that when it comes to real war, Americans cannot bear to see bullet-ridden bodies and headless corpses. If they were shown, moreover, the effect might be to weaken support for the war. In the case of Iraq, the conflict Americans saw was highly sanitized, with laser-guided weapons slamming into their intended targets with great precision. We observed this from afar, usually in pictures taken from bombers thousands of feet above their target, or in images of clouds of black smoke rising hundreds of yards away. Spared exposure to the victims of war, Americans had little idea of its human costs.

Next year, al-Jazeera plans to begin broadcasting in English. The images it shows may come as a shock to many Americans. In view of what they are usually shown, such a shock seems needed.

—*April 30, 2003*

23

As published in *The New York Review of Books*
February 26, 2004

NOW THEY TELL US

1. **IN RECENT MONTHS, US NEWS ORGANIZATIONS HAVE RUSHED** to expose the Bush administration's pre-war failings on Iraq. "Iraq's Arsenal Was Only on Paper," declared a recent headline in *The Washington Post*. "Pressure Rises for Probe of Prewar-Intelligence," said *The Wall Street Journal*. "So, What Went Wrong?" asked *Time*. In *The New Yorker*, Seymour Hersh described how the Pentagon set up its own intelligence unit, the Office of Special Plans, to sift for data to support the administration's claims about Iraq. And on "Truth, War and Consequences," a *Frontline* documentary that aired last October, a procession of intelligence analysts testified to the administration's use of what one of them called "faith-based intelligence."

Watching and reading all this, one is tempted to ask, where were you all before the war? Why didn't we learn more about these deceptions and concealments in the months when the administration was pressing its case for regime change—when, in short, it might have made a difference? Some maintain that the many analysts who've spoken out since the end of the war were mute before it. But that's not true. Beginning in the summer of 2002, the "intelligence community" was rent

25

by bitter disputes over how Bush officials were using the data on Iraq. Many journalists knew about this, yet few chose to write about it.

Before the war, for instance, there was a loud debate among intelligence analysts over the information provided to the Pentagon by Iraqi opposition leader Ahmed Chalabi and defectors linked to him. Yet little of this seeped into the press. Not until September 29, 2003, for instance, did The New York Times get around to informing readers about the controversy over Chalabi and the defectors associated with him. In a front-page article headlined "Agency Belittles Information Given by Iraqi Defectors," Douglas Jehl reported that a study by the Defense Intelligence Agency had found that most of the information provided by defectors connected to Ahmed Chalabi "was of little or no value." Several defectors introduced to US intelligence by the Iraqi National Congress, Jehl wrote, "invented or exaggerated their credentials as people with direct knowledge of the Iraqi government and its suspected unconventional weapons program."

Why, I wondered, had it taken the Times so long to report this? Around the time that Jehl's article appeared, I ran into a senior editor at the Times and asked him about it. Well, he said, some reporters at the paper had relied heavily on Chalabi as a source and so were not going to write too critically about him.

The editor did not name names, but he did not have to. The *Times*'s Judith Miller has been the subject of harsh criticism. *Slate, The Nation, Editor & Publisher*, the *American Journalism Review*, and the *Columbia Journalism Review* have all run articles accusing her of being too eager to accept official claims before the war and too eager to report the discovery of banned weapons after it.[1] Especially controversial has been Miller's alleged reliance on Chalabi and the defectors who were in touch with him. Last May, Howard Kurtz of *The Washington Post* wrote of an e-mail exchange between Miller and John Burns, then the *Times* bureau chief in Baghdad, in which Burns rebuked Miller for writing an article about Chalabi without informing him. Miller replied that she had been covering Chalabi for about ten years and had "done most of the stories about him for our paper." Chalabi, she added, "has provided most of the front page exclusives on WMD to our paper."

When asked about this, Miller said that the significance of her ties to Chalabi had been exaggerated. While she had met some defectors through him, she said, only one had resulted in a front-page story on WMD prior to the war. Her assertion that Chalabi had provided most of the *Times*'s front-page exclusives on WMD was, she said, part of "an angry e-mail exchange with a colleague." In the heat of such exchanges, Miller said,

"You say things that aren't true. If you look at the record, you'll see they aren't true."

This seems a peculiar admission. Yet on the broader issue of her ties to Chalabi, the record bears Miller out. Before the war, Miller wrote or co-wrote several front-page articles about Iraq's WMD based on information from defectors; only one of them came via Chalabi. An examination of those stories, though, shows that they were open to serious question. The real problem was relying uncritically on defectors of any stripe, whether supplied by Chalabi or not.

This points to a larger problem. In the period before the war, US journalists were far too reliant on sources sympathetic to the administration. Those with dissenting views—and there were more than a few—were shut out. Reflecting this, the coverage was highly deferential to the White House. This was especially apparent on the issue of Iraq's weapons of mass destruction— the heart of the President's case for war. Despite abundant evidence of the administration's brazen misuse of intelligence in this matter, the press repeatedly let officials get away with it. As journalists rush to chronicle the administration's failings on Iraq, they should pay some attention to their own.

2.

ON AUGUST 26, 2002, Vice President Dick Cheney gave a speech that was widely interpreted as signaling the administration's intention to wage war on Iraq. There "is no doubt," Cheney declared, that Saddam Hussein "has weapons of mass destruction" and is preparing to use them against the United States. Saddam, he said, not only had biological and chemical weapons but had "resumed his efforts to acquire nuclear weapons." If allowed to continue on this course, he added, Saddam could subject his adversaries to "nuclear blackmail." Accordingly, the United States had no choice but to take preemptive action against him.

The reference to nuclear weapons was especially telling. While Iraq was widely believed to have biological and chemical weapons, there was much more uncertainty regarding its nuclear program. In 1998, when UN inspectors left the country, it was generally agreed that Iraq's nuclear program had been dismantled. The question was, what had happened in the four years since? In his speech, Cheney flatly stated that Iraq had resumed its quest for a bomb, but neither he nor any other Bush official offered any supporting evidence.

At the time of Cheney's speech, *Times* reporters Judith Miller and Michael Gordon were investigating the state of Iraq's arsenal. Both had reported on Iraq for many years and brought certain perspectives to the assignment. Gordon, the paper's chief

29

military correspondent, had after the Gulf War teamed up with retired general Bernard Trainor to write *The Generals' War: The Inside Story of the Conflict in the Gulf* (1995). A detailed account of the military's conduct of the war, it strongly criticized the US decision to leave Saddam in power. From his many years of reporting on intelligence matters, Gordon knew how shocked US analysts had been after the Gulf War to find how far along Iraq had been in its effort to develop a nuclear weapon.

Miller, the coauthor of *Saddam Hussein and the Crisis in the Gulf* (1990) and *Germs: Biological Weapons and America's Secret War* (2001), was intimately acquainted with Saddam Hussein's genius for deception. In February 1998, she (together with William Broad) had written a 4,900-word report about Iraq's secret program to produce bioweapons and its success in concealing them from the outside world. According to the story, many former weapons inspectors and other experts with whom Miller and Broad talked believed that Baghdad "is still hiding missiles and germ weapons, and the means to make both."

Later that year, Miller met one of the first defectors who gave her information—Khidhir Hamza, a scientist who, until the late 1980s, had been a senior official in Iraq's nuclear program. After fleeing Baghdad in 1994, Hamza had made his way to Washington, where in 1997 he went to work for the Institute for Science and International Security, a small think tank, which arranged for Miller and fellow *Times* reporter James Risen to interview him. The result was a front-page story relating Hamza's account of the "inner workings" of Saddam's push for a bomb prior to the Gulf War, and recounting Hamza's belief that Saddam retained the infrastructure to duplicate that effort.

While seeing Hamza, Miller told me, she also was in touch with Ahmed Chalabi, and in 2001 he arranged for her to visit Thailand to interview another defector, a civil engineer named Adnan Ihsan Saeed al-Haideri. The resulting front-page story related al-Haideri's claim to have personally renovated "secret facilities for biological, chemical and nuclear weapons." These facilities were said to exist "in underground wells, private villas and under Saddam Hussein Hospital in Baghdad." Charles Duelfer, a former inspector, was quoted as saying that al-Haideri's account was consistent with other reports showing that Iraq had "not given up its desire" for WMD.

In 2002, Miller went to Turkey to interview yet another defector, Ahmed al-Shemri. A member of the Iraqi Officers Movement, another opposition group, al-Shemri (a pseudonym) claimed to have worked in Iraq's chemical weapons program, and he told Miller that Saddam had continued to produce VX and other chemical agents even while international inspectors were in Iraq. Iraq, he added, continued to store such agents at secret sites throughout the country.

By late summer of 2002, then, Miller had developed a circle of sources who claimed to have firsthand knowledge of Saddam's continued push for prohibited weapons. And as she and Gordon made the rounds of administration officials, they picked up a dramatic bit of information about Iraq's nuclear program. During the previous fourteen months, they were told, Iraq had tried to import thousands of high-strength aluminum tubes. The tubes had been intercepted, and specialists sent to examine them had concluded from their diameter, thickness, and other technical properties that they had only one possible use—as casings for rotors in centrifuges to enrich uranium, a key step in producing an atomic bomb.

This was dramatic news. If true, it would represent a rare piece of concrete evidence for Saddam's nuclear aspirations. And, on Sunday, September 8, 2002, the *Times* (then under the editorship of Howell Raines) led with the story, written by Miller and Gordon. "US Says Hussein Intensifies Quest for A-Bomb Parts," the headline said. The lead was emphatic:

> More than a decade after Saddam Hussein agreed to give up weapons of mass destruction, Iraq has

stepped up its quest for nuclear weapons and has embarked on a worldwide hunt for materials to make an atomic bomb, Bush administration officials said today.

Gordon and Miller went on to cite the officials' claims about the aluminum tubes and their intended use in centrifuges to enrich uranium.

The article contained several caveats, noting, for instance, that Iraq "is not on the verge of fielding a nuclear weapon." Overall, though, the language was stark:

> Mr. Hussein's dogged insistence on pursuing his nuclear ambitions, along with what defectors described in interviews as Iraq's push to improve and expand Baghdad's chemical and biological arsenals, have brought Iraq and the United States to the brink of war.

Administration "hard-liners," Gordon and Miller added, worried that "the first sign of a 'smoking gun'...may be a mushroom cloud." The piece concluded with a section on Iraq's chemical and biological weapons, relying heavily on the information supplied by Ahmed al-Shemri. "All of Iraq is one large storage facility," he was quoted as saying.

Gordon and Miller argue that the information about the aluminum tubes was not a leak. "The administration wasn't really ready to make its case publicly at the time," Gordon told me. "Somebody mentioned to me this tubes thing. It took a lot to check it out." Perhaps so, but administration officials were clearly delighted with the story. On that morning's talk shows, Dick Cheney, Colin Powell, Donald Rumsfeld, and Condoleezza Rice all referred to the information in the *Times* story. "It's now public," Cheney said on *Meet the Press*, that Saddam Hussein "has been seeking to acquire" the "kind of tubes" needed to build a centrifuge to produce highly enriched uranium, "which is what you have to have in order to build a bomb." On CNN's *Late Edition*, Rice said the tubes "are only really suited for nuclear weapons programs, centrifuge programs." She added: "We don't want the smoking gun to be a mushroom cloud"—a phrase lifted directly from the *Times*.

In the days that followed, the story of the tubes received wide publicity. And, on September 12, 2002, President Bush himself, in a speech to the UN General Assembly, said that "Iraq has made several attempts to buy high-strength aluminum tubes used to enrich uranium for a nuclear weapon"—evidence, he added, of its "continued appetite" for such a weapon. In the following months, the tubes would become a key prop in the administration's case for war, and the *Times* played a critical part in legitimizing it.

3.

FROM THE START, however, the *Times* story raised doubts among many nuclear experts. One was David Albright. A physicist and former weapons inspector who directed the Institute for Science and International Security (the same group for which the defector Khidhir Hamza had worked), Albright favored a tough position on Iraq, believing Saddam to have WMD and advocating strict measures to contain him. In the summer of 2001, however, after the aluminum tubes were intercepted, he had been asked by an official to find out some information about them, and in doing so he had learned of the doubts many experts had about their suitability for use in centrifuges. Some specialists with ties to the US Department of Energy and the International Atomic Energy Agency had concluded that the tubes were more likely destined for use in conventional artillery rockets, as Iraq itself had claimed. Officials at the State Department's Bureau of Intelligence and Research would later concur.

Reading the September 8 article, Albright felt it was important for the *Times* to take note of these dissenting views. In the past, he had worked frequently with Judith Miller; in fact, it was Albright who had arranged for her to interview Khidhir Hamza. Although he was unavailable when Miller tried to contact him for the September 8 story, he had several long conversations with her after it was published. He then described the doubts many centrifuge experts had about the administration's claims. And on September 13, 2002, a follow-up story appeared. It was not, however, what Albright had expected. Six paragraphs into an article that summarized the White House's case against Iraq, Miller and Gordon noted that senior officials acknowledged "that there have been debates among intelligence experts about Iraq's intentions in trying to buy such tubes." But, they quickly noted, those officials insisted that "the dominant view" in the administration was that the tubes were intended for use in centrifuges to enrich uranium. While some experts in the State and Energy Departments "had questioned whether Iraq might not be seeking the tubes for other purposes," the article stated,

> other, more senior, officials insisted last night that this was a minority view among intelligence experts and that the CIA had wide support, particularly among the government's top technical experts and nuclear scientists. "This is a footnote, not a split," a senior administration official said.

Yet Albright, having talked with a large number of those experts and scientists, knew that many did not support the CIA assessment. "Understanding the purpose of these tubes was very difficult," he told me.

> But hearing there's a debate in the government was knowable by a journalist. That's what I asked Judy to do—to alert people that there's a debate, that there are competent people who disagreed with what the CIA was saying. I thought for sure she'd quote me or some people in the government who didn't agree. It just wasn't there.

The *Times*, he added,

> made a decision to ice out the critics and insult them on top of it. People were bitter about that article—it says that the best scientists are with [the administration].

Miller rejects this. The article, she says, clearly stated that there was a debate about the tubes. As written, however, the piece gives far more attention and credence to officials who dismissed the dissenters, and the debate, as inconsequential—a "footnote."

Frustrated, Albright began preparing his own report about the tubes. Seeking an outlet, he approached Joby Warrick of *The*

Washington Post. In contrast to Miller and Gordon, Warrick had little experience covering national security matters; the environment was his beat. After the September 11 attacks, however, he was assigned to do investigative reporting related to the war on terrorism, and in the summer of 2002 he began looking into Iraq's weapons programs. Calling around to officials and former inspectors, he quickly discovered that "nobody knew very much." That, he told me, seemed particularly true of defectors. Francis Brooke, the Washington representative of the Iraqi National Congress, was constantly trying to give him information, but it never seemed to check out. "I became very frustrated at not being able to come up with anything solid showing that there were active weapons programs," Warrick said.

Albright's report about the aluminum tubes, however, seemed to offer an inside look at the debate within intelligence circles over Iraq's nuclear program.[2] Drawing on it, Warrick wrote an article describing how the administration's claims about the tubes were being challenged by "independent experts" who questioned whether they "were intended for a secret nuclear weapons program" or, as some believed, for use in conventional rockets. Warrick also noted reports that the Bush administration "is trying to quiet dissent among its own analysts over how to interpret the evidence." It was one of the first public mentions of the administration's possible misuse of the data on Iraq. Appearing on page A18, however, the story caused little stir.

4.

MEANWHILE, THE TUBES WERE DRAWING THE NOTICE of Knight Ridder's Washington bureau, which serves Knight Ridder's thirty-one newspapers in the US, including *The Philadelphia Inquirer*, *The Miami Herald*, and *The Detroit Free Press*. Almost alone among national news organizations, Knight Ridder had decided to take a hard look at the administration's justifications for war. As Washington bureau chief John Walcott recalled, in the late summer of 2002 "we began hearing from sources in the military, the intelligence community, and the foreign service of doubts about the arguments the administration was making." Much of the dissent came from career officers disturbed over the allegations being made by political appointees. "These people," he said, "were better informed about the details of the intelligence than the people higher up in the food chain, and they were deeply troubled by what they regarded as the administration's deliberate misrepresentation of intelligence, ranging from overstating the case to outright fabrication."

Walcott assigned two experienced reporters, Jonathan Landay and Warren Strobel, to talk with those sources. Drawing on them, Landay in early September 2002 filed a report for Knight Ridder that quoted senior US officials with access to intelligence on Iraq as saying that "they have detected no alarming increase in the threat that Iraqi dictator Saddam

Hussein poses to American security and Middle East stability."
While it was well known that Iraq was "aggressively trying to
rebuild" its weapons programs, Landay noted, "there is no
new intelligence that indicates the Iraqis have made significant
advances" in doing so.

In early October, Landay's curiosity was further aroused
when the CIA released a declassified version of its new
National Intelligence Estimate on Iraq. For the most part, the
document blandly summarized the agency's longstanding
findings regarding Iraq's ties to terrorists and its efforts to
develop WMD. In a brief section on the aluminum tubes, however, it noted that while the intelligence community as a whole
believed the tubes were intended for use in centrifuges, some
experts disagreed, believing they were intended for conventional weapons. This was a rare public acknowledgment of dissent within the intelligence agencies, and Landay, intrigued,
began making more calls. He eventually reached a veteran of
the US uranium enrichment program. "He'd been given data
on the tubes, and he said that this wasn't conclusive evidence,"
Landay recalled. In early October, Landay wrote about how the
CIA report had "exposed a sharp dispute among US intelligence experts" over Iraq's arsenal. One expert was quoted as
saying he did not believe the tubes were intended for use in

nuclear weapons because "their diameters were too small and the aluminum they were made from was too hard."

On October 8, 2002, Landay and Strobel, joined by bureau chief Walcott, filed a sharp account of the rising discontent among national security officers. "While President Bush marshals congressional and international support for invading Iraq," the article began, "a growing number of military officers, intelligence professionals and diplomats in his own government privately have deep misgivings about the administration's double-time march toward war." These officials, it continued,

> charge that administration hawks have exaggerated evidence of the threat that Iraqi leader Saddam Hussein poses—including distorting his links to the al-Qaida terrorist network.... They charge that the administration squelches dissenting views and that intelligence analysts are under intense pressure to produce reports supporting the White House's argument that Saddam poses such an immediate threat to the United States that pre-emptive military action is necessary.

As these reports show, there were many sources available to journalists interested in scrutinizing the administration's statements about Iraq. Unfortunately, however, Knight Ridder has no newspaper in Washington, D. C., or New York, and its stories did not get the national attention they deserved. But in mid-October, other news organizations began to pick up on some of the same discontent Knight Ridder had documented. *The Washington Post*, the Associated Press, *The Wall Street Journal*, *USA Today*, the *Los Angeles Times*, and the *Guardian* of London all ran articles raising questions about the administration's case for war. On October 10, *The New York Times* ran a front-page account by Michael Gordon of the divisions within the administration "over what intelligence shows about Iraq's intentions and its willingness to ally itself with al-Qaeda." And on October 24, the *Times*, again on its front page, reported that top Pentagon officials had set up a special intelligence unit to search for data to support the case for war. Written by Thom Shanker and Eric Schmitt, the article cited the concerns of some intelligence analysts that civilian policymakers were politicizing the intelligence to fit their hawkish position. The view "among even some senior intelligence analysts" at the CIA, they wrote, "is that Mr. Hussein is contained and is unlikely to unleash weapons of mass destruction unless he is attacked."

The unit referred to here was the Office of Special Plans, the same group Seymour Hersh would write about after the war.

As such reports show, its existence was widely known before the war. With many analysts prepared to discuss the competing claims over the intelligence on Iraq, the press was in a good position to educate the public on the administration's justifications for war. Yet for the most part, it never did so. A survey of the coverage in November, December, and January reveals relatively few articles about the debate inside the intelligence community. Those articles that did run tended to appear on the inside pages. Most investigative energy was directed at stories that supported, rather than challenged, the administration's case.

On December 12, for example, *The Washington Post* ran a front-page story by Barton Gellman contending that al-Qaeda had obtained a nerve agent from Iraq. Most of the evidence came from administration officials, and it was so shaky as to draw the attention of Michael Getler, the paper's ombudsman. In his weekly column, Getler wrote that the article had so many qualifiers and caveats that

> the effect on the complaining readers, and on me, is to ask what, after all, is the use of this story that practically begs you not to put much credence in it? Why was it so prominently displayed, and why not wait until there was more certainty about the intelligence?

And why, he might have added, didn't the *Post* and other papers devote more time to pursuing the claims about the administration's manipulation of intelligence? Part of the explanation, no doubt, rests with the Bush administration's skill at controlling the flow of news. "Their management of information is far greater than that of any administration I've seen," Knight Ridder's John Walcott observed. "They've made it extremely difficult to do this kind of [investigative] work." That management could take both positive forms—rewarding sympathetic reporters with leaks, background interviews, and seats on official flights—and negative ones—freezing out reporters who didn't play along. In a city where access is all, few wanted to risk losing it.

Such sanctions were reinforced by the national political climate. With a popular president promoting war, Democrats in Congress were reluctant to criticize him. This deprived reporters of opposition voices to quote, and of hearings to cover. Many readers, meanwhile, were intolerant of articles critical of the President. Whenever *The Washington Post* ran such pieces, reporter Dana Priest recalls, "We got tons of hate mail and threats, calling our patriotism into question." Fox News, Rush Limbaugh, and *The Weekly Standard*, among others, all stood ready to pounce on journalists who strayed, branding them liberals or traitors—labels that could permanently damage a career. Gradually, journalists began to muzzle themselves.

David Albright experienced this firsthand when, during the fall, he often appeared as a commentator on TV. "I felt a lot of pressure" from journalists "to stick to the subject, which was Iraq's bad behavior," Albright says. And that, in turn, reflected pressure from the administration: "I always felt the administration was setting the agenda for what stories should be covered, and the news media bought into that, rather than take a critical look at the administration's underlying reasons for war." Once, on a cable news show, Albright said that he felt the inspections should continue, that the impasse over Iraq was not simply France's fault; during the break, he recalls, the host "got really mad and chastised me."

"The administration created a set of truths, then put up a wall to keep people within it," Albright says. "On the other side of the wall were people saying they didn't agree. The media were not aggressive enough in challenging this."

5.

THE PRESS'S SUBMISSIVENESS WAS MOST APPARENT in its coverage of the inspections process. Responsibility for that process lay with two organizations: the International Atomic Energy Agency, which monitored Iraq's nuclear activities, and the United Nations Monitoring, Verification and Inspection Commission, which oversaw its biological and chemical programs. UNMOVIC, which was based in New York and headed by Hans Blix, got considerable coverage; the IAEA, which was based in Vienna and headed by Mohamed ElBaradei, got little.

"We were constantly frustrated," Melissa Fleming, an IAEA spokesperson, told me. "The whole focus was on UNMOVIC, which was in New York." According to IAEA staff members, the press gave far too much weight to what US experts or administration officials said. Jacques Baute, the head of the IAEA's Iraq inspection team, complained that the agency had a hard time getting its story out. And that story, he explained, was that by 1998 "it was pretty clear we had neutralized Iraq's nuclear program. There was unanimity on that."

The IAEA's success in dismantling Iraq's nuclear program was spelled out in the periodic reports it sent to the UN Security Council—reports that remained posted on its Web site. And, it was broadly agreed, any effort to restart that program after 1998 would have very likely been detected by the outside world. As the Carnegie Endowment noted in a recent report ("WMD in Iraq: Evidence and Implications"),

> Iraq's nuclear program had been dismantled by inspectors after the 1991 war, and these facilities—unlike chemical or biological ones—tend to be large, expensive, dependent on extensive imports, and very difficult to hide "in plain sight" under the cover of commercial (that is, dual-use) facilities.

These facts, it added, were "largely knowable" in the fall of 2002, when the debate over inspections was taking place.

Bush officials, however, were loudly proclaiming otherwise. "A return of inspectors would provide no assurance whatsoever of [Saddam's] compliance with UN resolutions," Vice President Cheney declared in his August 26 speech. "On the contrary, there is a great danger it would provide false comfort that Saddam was somehow 'back in his box.'"

Many journalists echoed this line. Seeking out former weapons inspectors for comment, they generally "gravitated to the most negative ones," Jacques Baute said. An example was David Kay. According to the IAEA, his background in nuclear and weapons matters was very limited—he has a Ph.D. in international affairs—and he spent no more than five weeks as an inspector in Iraq in 1991. This was far less time—and far longer ago—than was the case for many other inspectors.

Recently, Kay, after stepping down as the top US weapons investigator in Iraq, said that he thought Iraq had largely abandoned the production of illicit weapons during the 1990s and that one key reason was the tough UN inspections. Before the war, however, Kay often declared his contempt for inspections to reporters—including Judith Miller. On September 18, 2002, for instance, in an article headlined "Verification Is Difficult at Best, Say the Experts, and Maybe Impossible," Miller quoted a variety of officials and former inspectors about the nearly insurmountable obstacles inspectors would face if they returned to Iraq. David Kay, identified as "a former inspector who led the initial nuclear inspections in Iraq in the early 1990's," was quoted as saying of the inspectors that "their task is damn near a mission impossible." Miller also cited Khidhir Hamza, the defector she had written about in 1998. Identified as having "led part of Iraq's nuclear bomb program until he defected in 1994," he was quoted as estimating that "Iraq was now at the 'pilot plant' stage of nuclear production and within two to three years of mass producing centrifuges to enrich uranium for a bomb."

Iraq, he added, "now excelled" in hiding nuclear and other unconventional weapons programs.

In fact, Hamza never produced any convincing sources for these statements. Contrary to Miller's description, he had resigned from Iraq's nuclear program in 1990 and had no firsthand knowledge of it after the Gulf War. After coming to the United States, he had gone to work for David Albright's Institute for Science and International Security, but by 1999 his claims about Iraq's weapons programs had become so inflated that Albright felt he could no longer work with him, and Hamza left the institute. The following year he came out with a book, *Saddam's Bombmaker: The Terrifying Inside Story of the Iraqi Nuclear and Biological Weapons Agenda* (written with Jeff Stein), that, Albright says, "made many ridiculous claims." In light of this, he adds, he was surprised to see that Judith Miller continued to rely on Hamza. "Judy should have known about this," Albright says. "This is her area."

"Hamza had no credibility at all," one IAEA staff member told me. "Journalists who called us and asked for an assessment of these people—we'd certainly tell them." Miller said she believed Hamza was a credible source because he was very useful to the administration. After the war, she noted, the administration sent him to Iraq to work on atomic energy matters. Yet the administration's reliance on defectors like

51

Hamza was itself highly controversial and deserving of scrutiny. Few journalists provided it, though. In the months leading up to the war, Hamza was a popular source for journalists and a frequent guest on TV news shows. (In fairness, it should be noted that Judith Miller, along with Julia Preston, wrote an article for the *Times* in late January that, based on a two-hour interview with Hans Blix, described his differences with the Bush administration over its "assertions about Iraqi cheating" and "the notion that time was running out for disarming Iraq through peaceful means.")

In late November 2002, UN inspectors finally returned to Iraq. Shortly after, Iraq submitted to the UN a 12,000-page declaration stating it had no weapons of mass destruction. Iraq's failure to account for large stocks of banned weapons uncovered prior to 1998 fed suspicions that it still had such weapons. Nonetheless, IAEA inspectors felt confident that they could get a reliable reading of the status of Iraq's alleged nuclear program. They had more than a hundred sites they wanted to visit, based on interviews with defectors, data collected from previous inspections, satellite photos, and information provided by the CIA and other US intelligence agencies. Over the summer, IAEA specialists had detected in satellite photos new construction at sites where nuclear activity had taken place in the past. Visiting them, however, inspectors found no suspicious activity. The inspectors also took samples from rivers, canals, and lakes, testing for the presence of certain radioisotopes. None was found.

Finally, the inspectors investigated Iraq's attempted purchase of aluminum tubes. They examined rocket production and storage sites, studied tube samples, and interviewed key Iraqi personnel. From this they determined that the tubes were consistent with use in conventional rockets, as Iraq had maintained. On January 9, 2003, Mohamed ElBaradei issued a preliminary report on the inspectors' work. "To date," it noted,

> no new information of significance has emerged regarding Iraq's past nuclear programme (pre-1991) or with regard to Iraq activities during the period between 1991 and 1998. To date, no evidence of ongoing prohibited nuclear or nuclear-related activities has been detected, although not all of the laboratory results of sample analysis are yet available.

On the aluminum tubes, ElBaradei reported that they

> appear to be consistent with reverse engineering of

rockets. While it would be possible to modify such tubes for the manufacture of centrifuges, they are not directly suitable for it.

In short, the IAEA, after weeks of intensive inspections, had found no sign whatever of any effort by Iraq to resume its nuclear program. Given the importance the administration had attached to this matter, this would have seemed news of the utmost significance. Yet it was largely ignored. The *Times*, which had so prominently displayed its initial story about the aluminum tubes, buried its main article about ElBaradei's statement on page A10. (The paper did briefly mention ElBaradei's conclusion about the tubes in a front-page story that focused mainly on Iraq's lack of cooperation with the inspectors.) One of the few papers to give his statement significant treatment was *The Washington Post*. Following up on his earlier article on the tubes, Joby Warrick incorporated the IAEA findings into a detailed analysis of the claims and counterclaims surrounding the tubes. The article cited weapons inspectors, scientists, and other experts, all of whom cast strong doubt on the administration's arguments.[3]

The IAEA, Melissa Fleming observed, "was inundated with calls, but they were less of an investigative nature than about what the inspectors were finding on a daily basis. In general reporters showed little interest in more complex subjects like the aluminum tubes." Mark Gwozdecky, the IAEA's top spokesperson, added: "Nobody wanted to challenge the President. Nobody wanted to believe inspections had anything of value to bring to the table. The press bought into that."

6.

THE RECEPTION ACCORDED Mohamed ElBaradei's statement contrasted sharply with that given Colin Powell's speech at the United Nations on February 5, 2003. The secretary of state gave a high-tech presentation of intercepted tapes, satellite photos, videos, and diagrams to demonstrate what he called "a policy of evasion and deception" by Iraq dating back to 1991. Iraq's arsenal, Powell asserted, included mobile laboratories to produce bioweapons, unmanned aerial vehicles to deliver them, and chemical munitions plants. On the nuclear issue, Powell said that "Saddam Hussein is determined to get his hands on a nuclear bomb. He is so determined that he has made repeated covert attempts to acquire high-specification aluminum tubes from 11 countries, even after inspections resumed." Powell also asserted the existence of a "sinister nexus" between Iraq and al-Qaeda, citing as evidence the activities of Ansar al-Islam, a militant Islamic group based in northeastern Iraq. The group, he said, operated a poison-making camp in the region and had strong links to Iraqi intelligence.

The speech, while viewed skeptically by most foreign governments, received high approval ratings in American polls—and rapturous reviews from the American press. On CNN, after General Amer al-Saadi, Saddam Hussein's scientific adviser, appeared to offer a point-by-point rebuttal of Powell's charges, anchor Paula Zahn brought on former State Department spokesman James Rubin to comment. Introducing Rubin, Zahn said, "You've got to understand that most Americans watching this were either probably laughing out loud or got sick to their stomach. Which was it for you?"

"Well, really, both," Rubin replied. The American people "will believe everything they saw," he said. "They have no reason to doubt any of [Powell's] sources, any of the references to human sources, any of the pictures, or any of the intercepts."

The next day's *New York Times* carried three front-page articles on Powell's speech, all of them glowing. His presentation took "the form of a nearly encyclopedic catalog that reached further than many had expected," wrote Steven Weisman. According to Patrick Tyler, an "intelligence breakthrough" had made it possible for Powell "to set forth the first evidence of what he said was a well-developed cell of Al Qaeda operating out of Baghdad." The speech, he wrote, was "a more detailed and well-documented bill of particulars than many had expected."

The Washington Post was no less positive. "Data on Efforts to Hide Arms Called 'Strong Suit of Speech'" went one headline. "Agency Coordination Helps Yield Details on Al Qaeda 'Associate'" went another. In an editorial titled "Irrefutable," the paper asserted that, after Powell's performance, "it is hard to imagine how anyone could doubt that Iraq possesses weapons of mass destruction." The Op-Ed page ran four pieces about the speech—all of them full of praise. "An Old Trooper's Smoking Gun," stated the headline atop Jim Hoagland's column. Even the normally skeptical Mary McGrory pitched in with a favorable assessment, headlined "I'm Persuaded."

Tucked inside each paper, however, were articles that questioned the quality of Powell's evidence. In the *Times*, for instance, C. J. Chivers reported (on page A22) that Kurdish officials in northern Iraq were puzzled by Powell's claims of a poison-making facility in the area. A few days later, after visiting the purported camp, he found it to be a "wholly unimpressive place" that lacked even plumbing. In the *Post*, Joby Warrick raised questions about Powell's claims regarding the aluminum tubes. (This time, though, those questions were relegated to page A29.) *Newsweek* accompanied its article on the speech with five boxes evaluating Powell's key claims; each raised significant doubts. On his charge that Iraq had mobile biogerm labs, for instance, the magazine observed that experts believed such labs "would be all but unworkable" and that US intelligence, "after years of looking for them, has never found even one."

In the weeks following the speech, one journalist—Walter Pincus of *The Washington Post*—developed strong reservations about it. A longtime investigative reporter, Pincus went back and read the UN inspectors' reports of 1998 and 1999, and he was struck to learn from them how much weaponry had been destroyed in Iraq before 1998. He also tracked down General Anthony Zinni, the former head of the US Central Command, who described the hundreds of weapons sites the United States had destroyed in its 1998 bombing. All of this, Pincus recalled, "made me go back and read Powell's speech closely. And you could see that it was all inferential. If you analyzed all the intercepted conversations he discussed, you could see that they really didn't prove anything."

By mid-March, Pincus felt he had enough material for an article questioning the administration's claims on Iraq. His editors weren't interested. It was only after the intervention of his colleague Bob Woodward, who was researching a book on the war and who had developed similar doubts, that the editors agreed to run the piece—on page A17. Despite the administration's claims about Iraq's WMD, it began, "US intelligence agencies have been unable to give Congress or the Pentagon specific information about the amounts of banned weapons or where they are hidden...." Noting the pressure intelligence analysts were feeling from the White House and Pentagon, Pincus wrote that senior officials, in making the case for war, "repeatedly have failed to mention the considerable amount of documented weapons destruction that took place in Iraq between 1991 and 1998."

Two days later, Pincus, together with Dana Milbank, the *Post's* White House correspondent, was back with an even more critical story. "As the Bush administration prepares to attack Iraq this week," it began, "it is doing so on the basis of a number of allegations against Iraqi President Saddam Hussein that have been challenged—and in some cases disproved—by the United Nations, European governments and even US intelligence reports." That story appeared on page A13.[4]

The placement of these stories was no accident, Pincus says. "The front pages of *The New York Times*, *The Washington Post*, and the *Los Angeles Times* are very important in shaping what other people think," he told me. "They're like writing a memo to the White House." But the *Post's* editors, he said, "went through a whole phase in which they didn't put things on the front page that would make a difference."

7.

THE *POST* WAS NOT ALONE. The nearer the war drew, and the more determined the administration seemed to wage it, the less editors were willing to ask tough questions. The occasional critical stories that did appear were, like Pincus's, tucked well out of sight.

The performance of the *Times* was especially deficient. While occasionally running articles that questioned administration claims, it more often deferred to them. (The *Times*'s editorial page was consistently much more skeptical.) Compared to other major papers, the *Times* placed more credence in defectors, expressed less confidence in inspectors, and paid less attention to dissenters. The September 8 story on the aluminum tubes was especially significant. Not only did it put the *Times*'s imprimatur on one of the administration's chief claims, but it also established a position at the paper that apparently discouraged further investigation into this and related topics.

The reporters working on the story strongly disagree. That the tubes were intended for centrifuges "was the dominant view of the US intelligence community," Michael Gordon told me. "It looks like it's the wrong view. But the story captured what was and still is the majority view of the intelligence community—whether right or wrong." Not only the director of central intelligence but also the secretary of state decided to support it, Gordon said, adding:

> Most of the intelligence agencies in the US govern-
> ment thought that Iraq had something. Both Clinton
> and Bush officials thought this. So did Richard Butler,
> who had been head of UNSCOM and who wrote a
> book about Iraq called "The Greatest Threat." So it was
> a widely shared assumption in and out of government.
> I don't recall a whole lot of people challenging that.

Yet there were many people challenging the administration's
assertions. It's revealing that Gordon encountered so few of
them. On the aluminum tubes, David Albright, as noted above,
made a special effort to alert Judith Miller to the dissent surrounding them, to no avail.

Asked about this, Miller said that as an investigative reporter in
the intelligence area, "my job isn't to assess the government's
information and be an independent intelligence analyst myself.
My job is to tell readers of The New York Times what the government
thought about Iraq's arsenal." Many journalists would disagree
with this; instead, they would consider offering an independent
evaluation of official claims one of their chief responsibilities.

I asked Miller about her December 20, 2001, article about
Saeed al-Haideri, the Chalabi-linked defector who claimed that
Saddam Hussein had a network of hidden sites for producing

and storing banned weapons—sites said to include the ground under Saddam Hussein Hospital. In a subsequent piece about the Bush administration's use of defectors, Miller had stated that al-Haideri's interviews with US intelligence had "resulted in dozens of highly credible reports on Iraqi weapons-related activity and purchases." Yet neither UN inspectors nor the Iraq Survey Group was able to confirm any of those reports. Al-Haideri, Miller acknowledges, "might have been totally wrong, but I believe he was acting in good faith, and it was the best we could do at the time."

To this day, neither Miller nor the *Times* as a whole has reported on the failure to confirm al-Haideri's claims. Miller says that while the paper hasn't reported on al-Haideri's specific allegations, it did do "fifteen stories on weapons not found in Iraq." Yet, in view of the prominence the *Times* had given al-Haideri's claims, its failure to follow up on them suggests a lack of interest in correcting reports that were later contradicted by the evidence. (By contrast, the BBC show *Panorama*, which in September 2002 had reported some of al-Haideri's claims, noted pointedly in a follow-up program aired in November 2003 that the Iraq Survey Group had searched for but "found none of the laboratory facilities described by Mr. Haideri, including a bunker under a hospital.")

Looking back at her coverage of Iraq's weapons, Miller insists that the problem lies with the intelligence, not the reporting. "The fact that the United States so far hasn't found WMD in Iraq is deeply disturbing. It raises real questions about how good our intelligence was. To beat up on the messenger is to miss the point."

If nothing else, the Iraq saga should cause journalists to examine the breadth of their sources. "One question worth asking," John Walcott of Knight Ridder says, "is whether we in journalism have become too reliant on high-level officials instead of cultivating less glamorous people in the bowels of the bureaucracy." "In the case of Iraq," he added, the political appointees "really closed ranks. So if you relied exclusively on traditional news sources—assistant secretaries and above— you would not have heard things we heard." What Walcott calls "the blue collar" employees of the agencies—the working analysts or former analysts—were drawn on extensively by Knight Ridder, but by few others.

Since the end of the war, journalists have found no shortage of sources willing to criticize the administration. (Even Colin Powell, in a recent press conference, admitted that, contrary to his assertions at the United Nations, he had no "smoking gun" proof of a link between Saddam Hussein and al-Qaeda.) *The*

Washington Post has been especially aggressive in exposing the administration's exaggerations of intelligence, its inadequate planning for postwar Iraq, and its failure to find weapons of mass destruction. Barton Gellman, who before the war worked so hard to ferret out Iraq's ties to terrorists, has, since its conclusion, written many incisive articles about the administration's intelligence failures.[5]

The contrast between the press's feistiness since the end of the war and its meekness before it highlights one of the most entrenched and disturbing features of American journalism: its pack mentality. Editors and reporters don't like to diverge too sharply from what everyone else is writing. When a president is popular and a consensus prevails, journalists shrink from challenging him. Even now, papers like the *Times* and the *Post* seem loath to give prominent play to stories that make the administration look too bad. Thus, stories about the increasing numbers of dead and wounded in Iraq—both American and Iraqi—are usually consigned to page 10 or 12, where they won't cause readers too much discomfort.

—*January 29, 2004*

An updated version of an article published in *The New York Review of Books*
June 24, 2004

EPILOGUE: UNFIT TO PRINT?

"NOW THEY TELL US" elicited letters from several reporters and editors at The New York Times and The Washington Post. Robert Kaiser, an associate editor at the Post, wrote to question my assertion that while many journalists knew about the bitter disputes in the intelligence community over Iraq's WMD, few chose to write about them. According to Kaiser, this was not true of the Post. "We held nothing back that we knew," he wrote. Yes, he added, important stories "sometimes ran on the inside pages, but does Massing really mean to imply that editors who will run a story on A10 somehow lack courage if they won't put it on A1? That suggestion seems silly." Kaiser went on to give several examples of what he considered the Post's "tough" journalism in the lead-up to the war.

As for the Times, Judith Miller sent a brief letter that took issue with the wording of a single quote. Reporter James Risen asserted that he wrote several stories before the war that were critical of the Bush administration's case and that should have been mentioned in my article. And Michael Gordon, maintaining that I "cherry-picked the evidence" to bolster my case, went on at length about how the coverage of the WMD issue was "more complicated" than my article suggested. These letters, and my detailed responses, can be found in the March 25 and April 8, 2004, issues of *The New York Review*.

Since then, there have been several key developments related to my article and the debate it spurred. One is a revealing anecdote in Bob Woodward's new book, *Plan of Attack*. By mid-March 2003, Woodward writes, three separate sources had told him confidentially that the intelligence on Iraq's weapons of mass destruction "was not as conclusive as the CIA and the administration had suggested." This, he notes, "was troubling, particularly on what seemed to be the eve of war." When he mentioned this to Walter Pincus, a colleague at *The Washington Post*, Pincus told him that he had heard "precisely the same thing" from some of his sources. Woodward then drafted five paragraphs for a possible news story and gave a copy to Pincus and the *Post*'s national security editor. The draft began:

> Some of the key US intelligence that is the basis for the conclusion that Iraq has large caches of weapons of mass destruction looks increasingly circumstantial, and even shaky as it is further scrutinized, subjected to outside analysis and on-the-ground verification, according to informed sources.

A senior Bush administration source briefed last
month on the intelligence said it was "pretty thin,"
and might be enough to reach the legal standard
of "probable cause" to bring an indictment but not
enough for conviction.

Both Pincus and the editor thought the draft "a little strong,"
and Woodward agreed. "Though the sources were excellent,"
he wrote, "they were only saying the evidence was skimpy.
None were asserting that WMD would not be found in Iraq
after a war." Instead the *Post* on March 16, 2003, ran a much-
toned-down version by Pincus on page A17, under the headline "US Lacks Specifics on Banned Arms."

Looking back, Woodward writes,

I did not feel I had enough information to effectively
challenge the official conclusions about Iraq's alleged
WMD. In light of subsequent events, I should have
pushed for a front page story, even on the eve of war,
presenting more forcefully what our sources were saying.

This account reveals something about Woodward's method.
Like most of his other books, *Plan of Attack* contains much

information that, if disclosed in "real time," could have had an effect on the course of events. Woodward's books leave the impression that everything his subjects told him was embargoed until the book was ready for publication. In this case, however, Woodward was clearly free to reveal the doubts that some senior officials had expressed to him regarding the White House's claims about Iraq's arsenal. That he ultimately decided not to do so reinforces my own account of this episode in "Now They Tell Us" and contradicts Kaiser's assertion that the *Post* "held nothing back."[1]

On May 26, *The New York Times* published a lengthy editors' note belatedly acknowledging that the paper's pre-war coverage "was not as rigorous as it should have been." According to the note, which appeared at the bottom of page A10, accounts of Iraqi defectors were not analyzed with sufficient skepticism, and "articles based on dire claims about Iraq tended to get prominent display" while follow-up articles that called the original ones into question "were sometimes buried. In some cases, there was no follow-up at all." Without explicitly mentioning it, the note incorporated many of the criticisms made in "Now They Tell Us."

The *Times* deserves credit for running a detailed mea culpa. Yet the note seemed less than forthright. First, it did not cite the author of any of the articles. Rather, it laid the blame on "editors at several levels" who "should have been challenging reporters and pressing for more skepticism" but who "were perhaps too intent on rushing scoops into the paper." This was convenient for the *Times*, since some of those editors were part of Howell Raines's regime and have since departed. Nowhere did the note mention Judith Miller, who wrote or co-wrote four of the six main articles cited by the paper. Michael Gordon, whose byline appeared on two of them, was mentioned, but only as the author of a letter that he sent to *The New York Review* in response to my article—a letter that, the *Times* stated, "could serve as a primer on the complexities" of intelligence reporting. The note gave no hint that Gordon's own reporting has come in for serious questioning. Such an omission seems perplexing.

Four days after the editors' note appeared, Daniel Okrent, the *Times*'s public editor, who for months had said he would not address the *Times*'s coverage of WMD, finally did so. In a column sharply critical of the paper, he wrote that "some of the *Times*'s coverage" in the months leading up to the war "was credulous." "Much of it," he added, "was inappropriately italicized by lavish front-page display and heavy-breathing headlines," and "several fine articles" that provided perspective "were played as quietly as a lullaby." For the most part, Okrent's column echoed the editors' note. One of his few fresh points—that a "dysfunctional system" at the paper "enabled some reporters operating out of Washington and Baghdad to work outside the lines of customary bureau management"—was so vaguely worded as to lessen its impact. In one notable difference with the editors' note, Okrent named Judith Miller as the author of two highly questionable accounts. Yet Okrent, like the note, went out of his way to hold her blameless; "the failure" at the paper, he wrote, "was not individual, but institutional." This is entirely unpersuasive. Clearly, the failure was both individual and institutional. In light of the many serious questions raised about Miller's reporting, the determination by both the editors and the public editor to absolve her of any responsibility is mystifying and suggests the need for more outside reporting on what exactly is going on at the paper.

In their note, the Times's editors did promise "to continue aggressive reporting aimed at setting the record straight" on the story of Iraq's weapons. That's welcome. But the note's lack of candor does not inspire confidence. What's more, the paper's recent coverage of the war seems marred by some of the same flaws that were present in its pre-war reporting. This is apparent in its initial response to the Abu Ghraib scandal. When 60 Minutes II aired photos of US soldiers committing abuses at the prison in Iraq, the images quickly flashed around the world. On the next day, Thursday, April 29, the Times ran a modest story about the abuses that appeared at the bottom of page A15; none of the photos appeared. By Friday, the photos were receiving heavy play in both the European press and on Arab satellite TV; in the United States, The Washington Post, The Baltimore Sun, Newsday, and the New York Daily News all ran at least one of the photos. The Times, by contrast, ran no article and published no photos.

A day later, on Saturday, May 1, the scandal made the Times's front page. "Bush Voices 'Disgust' at Abuse of Iraqi Prisoners" ran the headline atop a story about the President's comments, made in the White House Rose Garden. In other words, the Times's initial front-page story on Abu Ghraib concentrated not on the abuses themselves but on the President's response to them. And no photo of the abuses appeared on the front page. One had to jump, along with the story, to page A5 to see two of the photos. The article, which described the furor the photos had caused around the world, contained a quote from the Times's executive editor, Bill Keller, explaining why the Times had not run them earlier. The paper's news desk, Keller said, had held off because it "could not, in the time available, ascertain their authenticity."

This seems dubious. Two days earlier, the *Times*, in its initial article about the scandal, had specifically noted that the photos shown on CBS had been verified by military officials. A survey of the paper's recent coverage of Iraq suggests that something deeper is at work. For months, the *Times* has seemed slow to recognize important news developments out of Iraq and to give them the attention they deserve. Aside from the Abu Ghraib scandal, which has lately taken over the *Times*'s coverage, the paper has seemed intent on keeping bad news off the front page, especially when it reflects poorly on the Bush administration. Some examples:

• On May 5, the Bush administration announced that it was going to request $25 billion more for operations in Iraq and Afghanistan. This came six months after Congress had approved $87 billion for such operations on the assurance from the administration that that amount would last through the end of 2004. The new request was yet another sign that the war was proving far more costly than originally forecast, and *The Washington Post* announced the news in a two-column headline on its front page ("$25 Billion More Sought to Fund Wars; White House Hoped to Delay Request until After Election"). In the *Times*, though, the news received a one-sentence "reefer" on its front page, directing readers to a ho-hum account on page A22. "Lawmakers," it blandly noted, "said they expected to comply with the request." It was not until May 14, after a contentious hearing at which senators from both parties attacked the administration's request, that the *Times* felt the story was fit for its front page.

• On May 7, *The Wall Street Journal* carried an explosive front-page report revealing that the Red Cross in February had sent the Bush administration a report detailing widespread abuses against Iraqi prisoners by US military intelligence personnel. According to the *Journal*, the twenty-four-page report presented a portrait of prisoner treatment "that is at odds with statements by administration officials that abuse wasn't condoned by military commanders and was limited to a handful of low-ranking soldiers." Normally, such reports are kept confidential; the *Journal*'s disclosure of its contents marked a critical moment in the unfolding of the scandal, and the news made front pages around the world. Not in the *Times*, however. Not until May 11 did it run a modest story summarizing the report's findings, tucked away on page A11. Readers reliant on the *Times* would have had a hard time understanding the huge impact the document has had.

• On May 9, *The Washington Post* ran an eye-catching front-page article by Thomas Ricks on rising dissent among senior US military officers over the Bush administration's conduct of the war. One senior general told Ricks that the United States is already on the road to defeat. Other officers said that "a profound anger is building within the Army" with Donald Rumsfeld, "whom they see as responsible for a series of strategic and tactical blunders over the past year." The *Times* had nothing at all comparable, on this or any other day. It did, however, find space on that day's front page for a reassuring piece about how US brands like Ford and Coca-Cola were continuing to sell well abroad despite international disapproval of US actions in Iraq.

The *Times* does show flashes of independent reporting. On April 28, for instance, it ran an incisive front-page piece by Eric Schmitt on how the US siege of Fallujah was a "case study in mistaken assumptions, dashed hopes, rivalry between the Army and the Marine Corps, and a tragedy that became a trigger...." And, as the prison scandal unfolded, the *Times*—mobilizing its staff—produced many revealing accounts, including a May 13 piece on the harsh methods used by the CIA to interrogate top al-Qaeda figures, and several vivid reports by Ian Fisher about former Iraqi prisoners who had been horribly treated at the hands of US guards. As this shows, the *Times* remains adept at "flooding the zone," in the phrase of former executive editor Howell Raines, offering many dramatic reports about a story once it's been ratified as important. And the paper's editorials have been withering about US actions in Iraq. In general, however, the *Times* has seemed cautious and complacent. With few exceptions, its editors have purged the front page of any signs of blood or death; reports of US casualties are usually relegated to inside pages, and photos seem selected more for their visual appeal than for what they might reveal about the terrible realities of war.

The leisureliness of the *Times*'s coverage is especially apparent when compared to that of its top competitor. In recent months, *The Washington Post* has stood out among US news organizations for its sharp and insightful reporting, in both Washington and Baghdad. Hardly a day goes by that the *Post* does not publish some revealing story about conflicts within the Bush administration, debates within the intelligence world, Coalition policies in Iraq, and the relations among that country's ethnic, religious, and tribal groups. During the prison scandal, the *Post* ran an eye-opening three-part series ("The Road to Abu Ghraib") on the abuses that had occurred not only in Iraq but also in Guantánamo, Afghanistan, and Qatar—part of a "worldwide constellation" of secret US detention centers.

When it comes to Iraq, the rivalry between the *Times* and the *Post* has become "A Tale of Two Papers," the one late and lethargic, the other astute and aggressive.

Even the *Post*, though, has had its problems. In his May 9 column, Michael Getler, the paper's ombudsman, chided it for being "slow off the mark" on the Abu Ghraib story. As he observed, the US Central Command back on January 16 had disclosed in a news release that an investigation had been opened into reports of detainee abuse at a Coalition detention facility. That same week, CNN reported that there were photos of abuses. It was not until after the story broke on *60 Minutes II*, more than three months later, however, that the *Post* ran with it, Getler wrote.

So, even as the coverage of Iraq has grown sharper, the US press has shied away from showing the full realities on the ground there. This, in turn, reflects some important structural limitations in the approach of American journalists to the war.

2.

IN EARLY APRIL, when fighting broke out in Fallujah, US correspondents, regarding the city as too dangerous to enter, embedded themselves with US Marine units encamped there. This practice, popular during the invasion, has been revived amid the surging violence in Iraq. In return for protection by the Marines, embedded correspondents agree to abide by certain ground rules, such as not reporting on US combat deaths. One correspondent, Pamela Constable of *The Washington Post*, described her experience in an article for the paper's "Style" section. Along with seven other correspondents, Constable wrote, she hunkered down with a Marine battalion in a deserted factory filled with empty bottles of soda pop. "I quickly became part of an all-American military microcosm," she wrote. During the day, she could move about only with the Marines. At night, she listened to the "terrifying sounds" of helicopter gunships, high-flying bombers, and insurgent mortar rounds. "After each attack," she wrote,

> I strained to listen for signs of humanity in the darkened city. I imagined holocaust—city blocks in flames, families running and screaming. But the only sounds were the baying of frightened dogs and the

indecipherable chanting of muezzins, filling the air with a soft cacophony of Koranic verse.

The fighters inside the city "remained invisible," and the local population was "frustratingly beyond our reach," Constable wrote.

> We knew people were running out of food, and we heard rumors of clinics flooded with the dead and wounded. But the few Fallujans we encountered were either prisoners with handcuffed wrists and hooded heads, or homeowners waiting sullenly for their houses to be searched, or refugees timidly approaching military checkpoints with white flags.... Sometimes on patrols, people approached us reporters and pleaded for help in Arabic, but there was nothing we could do.

Al-Jazeera, by contrast, had a correspondent and crew inside the city, and several times a day they were filing dramatic reports of the fighting. According to their accounts, the US bombing was causing hundreds of civilian casualties plus extensive physical destruction. As for what Constable took to be the Koranic chantings of the muezzins, Arabic speakers could tell that these were actually urgent appeals for ambulances and calls on the local population to rise up and fight the Americans. So while Arab viewers were getting independent (if somewhat sensationalized) reports from the field, Americans were getting their news filtered through the Marines.

I don't mean to single out Constable, who is a fine reporter, and who has filed many insightful reports. Rather, her dispatch captures the problems US journalists as a whole face in Iraq today. First and foremost is security. The recent upsurge in violence has turned much of Iraq into a no-go zone for US news organizations, and American reporters have found it difficult to leave Baghdad (and in some cases their hotels). To try to compensate, US news organizations have relied increasingly on Iraqi journalists, who are able to move about more freely, especially in conflicted areas. Even they, though, have faced growing hostility and threats.[2] In covering a volatile place like Fallujah, many US correspondents have chosen to become embedded with the military. One result is severely limited access. As Constable noted, she could see little of what was going on inside the city, had little contact with those fighting the US, and could not determine the impact the fighting was having on local residents. Compounding the problem was her lack of knowledge of Arabic—a handicap shared by all but a handful of US correspondents. As a result, the muezzin chants were "indecipherable."

Apart from such practical considerations, however, US news organizations in Iraq suffer from a more engrained problem. As American institutions covering an American occupation, they generally share certain premises and presumptions about the conflict. Even as reporters rush to chronicle Iraqi resentment of the occupation, they still tend to frame the conflict in much the same way that US officials do. Often, American journalists seem embedded with the military not only physically but also mentally.

Consider, for example, a recent NPR interview between Sunday morning host Liane Hansen and Tony Perry, a correspondent in Iraq for the *Los Angeles Times*. With Fallujah still tense, Perry had decided to embed with a Marine unit that had taken over a decrepit public housing project on the outskirts of town. The Marines had forced out its residents, and Perry described how "spooky" it was to stay in the grimy, trash-strewn apartment amid the ghostlike relics of the family that had been living there. To make up for its takeover of the building, Perry said, the United States was planning to spend a half-million dollars on repairs and reconstruction:

They're going to build a soccer field for the kids. . . .

They're going to spruce up a school nearby. So we are trying to make amends by money. I'm never quite sure how great an apology money is when you've uprooted people and made them flee from their homes, but the US is going to do the best it can.

As for the people who had lived in the unit in which he was staying, Perry said, the Marines had given them $200 and would give them more when they returned. Feeling guilty, Perry said, he had himself left "a few bucks" under a Mr. Potato Head doll that was still sitting on a TV set. "Did you say you put the money under the Mr. Potato Head doll?" Hansen asked, perking up. Yes, Perry said, explaining that looters would be less likely to find it there.

Where, Hansen asked, had the family gone? "They fled into rural areas," Perry said. "These are tribal people, so they have connections, extended families. I think they all found ways to live and survive in this environment." A lot had cars,

so they weren't thrown down the road and put in some refugee camps. They found places to hunker down. It also took them out of the way of the fighting. Don't forget that once the Marines moved in, the insurgents

83

were rocketing and mortaring this location, so it got them out of the way, too, for their own safety.

So, in Perry's telling, the Marines, in driving the family from their home, were actually doing it for their own good. And, happily, the family was able to flee to rural areas and stay with tribal relatives rather than be forced into a refugee camp. What's more, the Marines—"we," as Perry put it—were going to "make amends" by sprucing up the area and building a soccer field. Perry, unable to move about the city and talk with Iraqis, could only pass on optimistic, reassuring speculation that those displaced would "live and survive." Sharing quarters with the Marines, Perry seemed to share their outlook as well.

After listening to that interview, I looked up some of Perry's stories in the *Los Angeles Times*. They were markedly solicitous of the Marines. Some headlines: "Goodwill-Hunting Marines Set Their Sights on Refurbishing Mosques"; "Marines on a Mission to Win Friends in Iraq: Armed with Toys and Candy for the Children and Seeds and Farm Tools for the Adults, US Troops Reach Out to Villagers near Fallouja"; "Where There's Battle, There's Bravery —and Recognition: Several Marines in Iraq are Candidates for Citations." None of these articles, by the way, gave any indication that Perry had written them while embedded with the Marines.

To alert readers, the articles should perhaps have carried, after the correspondent's name, a tag like "Embedded with US Forces." In this respect, though, Perry's dispatches are not unusual— few American papers use such truth-in-advertising labels.

In Washington, too, a similar form of mental embedding seems at times to have taken place. On April 29, for instance, *The New York Times* ran a front-page piece about a Pentagon study on the composition of the insurgent forces inside Iraq. This had been the subject of much debate. Were the insurgents part of an indigenous resistance to the US occupation? Or were they hard-core elements intent on sabotaging any effort to bring democracy to Iraq? The Pentagon's report claimed they were the latter, and the *Times* respectfully summarized it. "Hussein's Agents Behind Attacks, Pentagon Finds," the head-line stated. (Note the choice of words—"finds," rather than the more objective "claims" or "says.") According to the Pentagon, the attacks in Fallujah and elsewhere "are organized and often carried out by members of Saddam Hussein's secret service, who planned for the insurgency even before the fall of Baghdad," the *Times* reported. Overall, it added, the Pentagon estimated there were 1,500 to 2,000 "hard-core insurgents, including members of the Iraqi Special Republican Guard who melted away under the American-led offensive...."

The report on the Pentagon study clearly should have included some independent analysis. But the *Times*, happy with its "scoop," offered none.

"American officials have given seven or eight different reasons for why people are fighting the US," I was told by Rami Khouri, the executive editor of *The Daily Star* newspaper in Beirut, which is carried as an insert in the *International Herald Tribune* throughout the Middle East. "They've said they're dead-enders, former Baathists, former army people, Islamic terrorists, people sneaking in from the border with Syria, a bunch of thugs aligned with Moqtada al-Sadr. It's amazing that a country like Iraq can produce so many different types of people who want to kill Americans. This analysis is something that deeply offends people here. Yet the American press by and large accepts it. They're way too compliant with the Pentagon and White House views."

Khouri added: "You don't need to be in Fallujah to understand Fallujah. The people there don't like being occupied or dictated to by a foreign power, even if that power is coming to liberate them."

Such an analysis may be too schematic. In May, *Newsweek*'s Joshua Hammer got a rare firsthand glimpse of the insurgents when, venturing into Fallujah, he and a photographer were seized by three armed men, who drove them to a house in a back alley for questioning. After convincing his captors that he was a journalist and not a CIA agent, Hammer learned that one of them was a former university student who had originally supported the invasion but turned against the United States after it became an occupying power. As this young man explained it, the Americans were facing two types of adversaries in Fallujah—ordinary Iraqis like himself who opposed the American occupation, and a mix of foreign fighters and hard-line local jihadis with an "inflexible hatred of the West." As this suggests, the forces arrayed against the United States consist of disparate elements, and this makes generalization difficult.

That Hammer had to be seized at gunpoint to find this out shows just how dangerous Iraq has become for US correspondents. And things have only gotten worse as the fighting has spread to Najaf, Karbala, and other points in the Shiite south. US journalists have generally been unable to see the fighting up close. But, as Khouri suggests, the problem is as much one of attitude as of access.

As the fighting in the south escalated, I spoke with Youssef Ibrahim, one of the few journalists of Arab descent to have worked for a major US news organization. Raised in Egypt, Ibrahim spent twenty-four years with The New York Times and The Wall Street Journal, many of them covering the Middle East. After working as a consultant for BP, he became a senior fellow at the Council on Foreign Relations. I spoke with him soon after he had arrived in Dubai, where he now writes for Gulf News, among other publications. While he was in New York, Ibrahim told me, he was able to see al-Jazeera only on its Web site; in Dubai, he can watch it live, and, even as we spoke, he said, it was showing daily reports of the heavy fighting in Najaf and Karbala.

"There's nothing of this on CNN, let alone Fox or MSNBC," he said. "Right now I'm watching a gunfight in Najaf. They're filming it themselves, without being embedded with American troops. Now they've switched to Baghdad—they have [a team] reporting from Sadr City, which has 2.5 million people. If I flip to CNN, they'll give a report from Baghdad about the day's goings-on in Iraq, as seen by Americans with a Marine unit. As a professional American reporter, I feel that's not the way we are trained to do our job."

Asked if he felt al-Jazeera is balanced, Ibrahim said of course not. "It's our equivalent of Fox News," he said, "but it's our Fox News. It gives me the other side of the story." Americans rarely get to see the other side.

The confrontation between the US military and the Mahdi

Army of Moqtada al-Sadr has been of profound importance for the US occupation. Al-Sadr's strategy seemed clear—to provoke the Americans into attacking the Shiite holy places. If that happened, much of the Muslim world might react. Yet the coverage in the US was thin and uninformative. Consumed by the ongoing Abu Ghraib scandal, US news organizations seemed to have little interest in the fighting and its political ramifications. And what did appear seemed one-sided. On CNN, for instance, I saw the correspondent Jane Arraf, speaking from a US Army base in Najaf, offering assurances that the US military was "acting with surprising restraint." General Martin Dempsey, the commanding officer of the First Army Division, told Arraf that his troops were engaging in "precise" fire in the city. "We're going to honor the sanctity of religious sites," he reassuringly said. There was no one to comment on how local Iraqis saw the fighting.

Similarly, The New York Times's coverage of the fighting in the south has relied heavily on US military sources. Stories carrying a "Karbala" dateline seem reported in large part from a US military encampment several miles outside the city. Over and over, the Times quotes US commanders giving precise figures of the number of insurgents killed—an eerie throwback to the body-count days of Vietnam. The photos from Karbala appearing in the Times are mostly of GIs in heroic poses; few show the heavy damage inflicted on the city by the recent fighting.

It's important to note that US news organizations have run many excellent stories about Iraq and the US presence there. And they have done so in the face of grave danger. But that danger, and the restrictions on access it has imposed, demand new approaches to news gathering. In order to convey a full picture of what's happening inside Iraq, US news outlets could as a first step incorporate more reporting and footage from international news organizations. Al-Jazeera, al-Arabiya, and other Arabic-language TV stations have a wide presence on the ground. European outlets like the BBC, the *Guardian*, *The Financial Times*, and *Le Monde* have Arabic-speaking correspondents with close knowledge of the Middle East; Reuters, the Associated Press, and Agence France-Presse have many correspondents stationed in places where US organizations do not. It's remarkable how little reporting from these organizations makes its way into American news accounts.

In the current climate, of course, any use of Arab or European material—no matter how thoroughly edited and checked—could elicit charges of liberalism and anti-Americanism. The big question is, have US news organizations achieved the necessary independence and nerve to withstand it?

—*June* 30, 2004

NOTE TO "THE UNSEEN WAR"

1 "The Fall of Baghdad," May 15, 2003.

NOTES TO "NOW THEY TELL US"

1 See Jack Shafer, "The *Times* Scoops That Melted," *Slate*, July 25, 2003; Russ Baker, "'Scoops' and Truth at the *Times*," *The Nation*, June 23, 2003; William E. Jackson Jr., "Miller's Latest Tale Questioned," *Editor & Publisher Online*, September 23, 2003, at www.editorandpublisher.com; Charles Layton, "Miller Brouhaha," *AJR*, August/September 2003; and John R. MacArthur, "The Lies We Bought," *CJR*, May/June 2003.

2 See "Aluminum Tubing Is an Indicator of an Iraqi Gas Centrifuge Program: But Is the Tubing Specifically for Centrifuges?" *ISIS*, updated October 9, 2002, at www.isis-online.org.

3 See also Bob Drogin and Maggie Farley, "After 2 Months, No Proof of Iraq Arms Programs," *Los Angeles Times*, January 26, 2003, for a thorough account of how UN inspectors were "unable to corroborate Bush administration claims" about Iraq's weapons.

4 See Harry Jaffe, "Why Doesn't the *Post* Love Walter Pincus?" *The Washingtonian*, September 2003, and Ari Berman, "The Postwar *Post*," TheNation.com, September 17, 2003.

5 See, especially, "Depiction of Threat Outgrew Supporting Evidence," August 10, 2003, p. A1. Co-written with Walter Pincus, the article describes in impressive detail how the administration twisted the intelligence on the aluminum tubes.

NOTES TO "UNFIT TO PRINT?"

1 Kaiser is further contradicted by the *Post*'s ombudsman, Michael Getler, who, in a June 20, 2004, column, criticized the paper's coverage in the months before the war on two grounds: "(1) Too many *Post* stories that did challenge the official administration view appeared inside the paper rather than on the front page; and (2) too many public events in which alternative views were expressed, especially during 2002, when the debate was gathering steam, were either missed, underreported or poorly displayed."

2 See "Under Threat: Iraqi Journalists Frequently Face Hazardous Conditions on the Job," by Joel Campagna and Hani Sabra, Committee to Protect Journalists, at www.cpj.org.

The New York Review of Books